José Micaelson Lacerda Morais

Capitalism and the Value Revolution:

apogee and annihilation

Copyright © José Micaelson Lacerda Morais, 2022.

Translated from the Brazilian edition *O capitalismo e a revolução do valor: apogeu e aniquilação.* Independently published, 2021.

Text Review
Núcleo de Línguas da Universidade Regional do Cariri – NUCLIN.
Reviewers: Larisse Carvalho de Oliveira, Martt Magna Antero, Shalatiel Bernardo Martins, Tomás Almeida Costa.

Capitalism and the revolution of value: apogee and annihilation / José Micaelson Lacerda Morais. Independently published, 2022.

1. Political economy 2. Value 3. Surplus value 4. Capital 5. Capitalism

For all who still believe in the possibility of building a human society free of exploitation among social subjects.

"APOLOGIST CONCEPTION OF THE PRODUCTIVITY OF ALL PROFESSIONS" ACCORDING TO MARX

"[...] The criminal produces not only crimes but also criminal law, and with this also the professor who gives lectures on criminal law and in addition to this the inevitable compendium in which this same professor throws his lectures onto the general market as 'commodities'. This brings with it argumentation of national wealth, quite apart from the personal enjoyment which – as a competent Witness, Herr Professor Roscher, [tells] us – the manuscript of the compendium brings to its originator himself [...] The criminal moreover produces the whole of the police and of criminal justice, constables, judges, hangmen, juries, etc.; and all these different lines of business, which form equally many categories of the social division of labour, develop different capacities of the human spirit, create new needs and new ways of satisfying them. Torture alone has given rise to the most ingenious mechanical inventions and employed many honourable craftsmen in the production of this instruments [...] The criminal produces an impression, partly moral and partly tragic, as the case may be, and in this way renders a 'service' by arousing the moral and aesthetic feelings of the public. He produces not only compendia on Criminal Law, not only penal codes and along with them legislators in this field, but also art, belles-lettres, novels, and even tragedies [...] The criminal breaks the monotony and everyday security of bourgeois life [...] Thus he gives a stimulus to the productive forces [...] The effects of the criminal on the development of productive power can be shown in detail. Would locks ever have reached their present degree of excellence had there been no thieves? Would the making of banknotes have reached its present perfection had there been no forgers? Would the microscope have found its way into the sphere of ordinary commerce (see Babbage) but for trading frauds? Doesn't practical chemistry owe just as much to adulteration of commodities and the efforts to show it up as to the honest zeal for production? Crime, through its constantly new methods of attack on property, constantly calls into being new methods of defense, and so it is as productive as strikes for the invention of machines [...]".

Karl Marx, Theories of Surplus Value (vol.1).

Summary

1. INTRODUCTION   9

2. THE VALUE REVOLUTION   25

2.1. Smith and the value   25
    2.1.1. The natural price of salary   39

2.2. The value in Marx   43

2.3. Productive labour and surplus value   63

3. THE METAMORPHOSES OF VALUE AND SURPLUS VALUE   71

3.1 Value, surplus value and automation   80

3.2. Destruction of the labour world   97

3.3. The autonomy of self-determination of capital   101

4. HEIGHT AND ANNIHILATION OF HUMANITY   120

5. REFERENCES   127

1. Introduction

"Economic servitude" was one of the terms used by Marx in book I of Capital to designate the condition of continuous exploitation of the wage worker under. The capitalist process of production "[...] it thereby reproduces and perpetuates the condition for exploiting the labourer. It incessantly forces him to sell his labour-power in order to live and enables the capitalist to purchase labour-power in order that he may enrich himself [...]" (MARX, 2017a, p. 652). Thus, the production and reproduction of its own social relationship (capitalists, on the one hand, salaried workers, on the other) is perpetuated indefinitely in capitalist time. There would be no major problems if this relationship did not involve the private appropriation of socially performed production. If profit, interest, wage and income of the land, constitute equal proportions of total social income, thus also providing equal purchasing power for each of the social subjects. If the economic surplus were used to provide the same conditions and levels, housing, health, leisure, transportation, education, etc.; in short, social and economic infrastructure for every human being. In other words, if capitalist social relations were not based on the exploitation of social labour. After all, we are all human beings who, regardless of race, creed, color and place, have equal social needs, so that all lives should matter.

In capitalism, in general, the wage worker, direct producer of the totality of social production, only a proportion of the product is no more than sufficient for its reproduction. He as a human being is not entitled to the social benefits resulting from his own labour. Only the duty to reproduce itself as a labour force, regardless of how much material wealth its various generations, whether in the form of slave, servant or wage worker, have produced on the face of the earth. The capitalist, however, has a different income called profit, an income that is derived from social production, which should benefit social subjects equally, but which becomes a particular privilege of fruition of the benefits of material wealth. It is not because a person is smarter or more entrepreneurial than others that he should appropriate both labour and the fruit of the labour of others. In terms of common sense, it's not because a person is the strongest of all that they should get everyone's food for themselves. In this case, the only difference between instinct and intelligence (reason), would be that the first is an innate characteristic of nature and the second a characteristic of the evolution of a peculiar animal, the human being (and the consequent formation and development of human society). However, both would have the same purpose: the creation of an advantage of one over the other (in nature, survival, in human society, exploitation of social labour). So far this has shown the essence of social organization that we have built throughout history, the foundation of real economics and Economic Science.

Economic history is the history of exploitation forms of social labour, from ancient slavery, through feudalism, to capitalism. The development of economics as a science, even our current historical block, is both the way of justifying and creating more efficient and alienating ways of exploiting social labour. One of the greatest virtues of our reason (intelligence) has been to expose this essence (the foundation of our form of social organization) of the exploitation of social labour. Marx with his theory of value and surplus value can still be considered the author of the authors. Our greatest difficulty has been accepting that we can achieve a different form of sociability, even in the face of the immense social inequality achieved at the global level and the imminent collapse of the planet's natural resources. In the thesis, the meaning of reason should be to give the human being, as a social subject, the ability to establish social relationships differentiated from the relationships existing between other living beings in nature (food chain). However, a society that bases its organization on the labour exploitation, concentrates social wealth in the hands of the few, differentiates its population between rich and poor, elects a mere representation (money) as a meaning of life, transforms people into commodities and commodities into subjects of affection and distinction and does nothing more than reproducing a social representation of the food chain of nature. The richness and distinction of some depend on the exploitation and expropriation of the labour of many, in short, on the theft of many hours of life of their fellowmen.

Capitalism, while freed the individual from feudal servitude, also created a new form of servitude. However, under the guise of that individual's legal freedom, "[...] the labourer belongs to capital before he has sold himself to capital. His economic bondage is both brought about and concealed by the periodic sale of himself, by his change of masters, and by the oscillations in the market-price of labour-power" (MARX, 2017a, p. 652-653).

Economic servitude in capitalism is directly associated with a specific form of value and its contradictions. At the same time both are covered and evidenced in the exchange value, which are expressed in a social relationship, also specific, the capital-value, which, in turn, is based on the separation of the direct producer from its means of production and subsistence (proletarianization process) and the concentration of these means in the hands of a small class (capitalists who have the total means of production and subsistence of society).

In turn, value is a word that holds numerous meanings by (and among) various areas, such as economics, law, mathematics, music, logic, philosophy, painting, etc. Generically, value can represent both an intrinsic property to an object or individual and can express a relationship between objects and individuals. When we affirm the square root value of 4 as equal to 2, this result represents an intrinsic value derived from the formula itself. Likewise, when we affirm that a person has great value, we relate this term to certain qualities proper to the individual, such as courage or patience, for example. Value as an expression of a relationship (whether social or comparison between objects) always presents itself as a result derived from attributes and processes that occurred or occur in the interaction between objects and individuals and between them. This is because every relationship implies the past or present existence of the comparison of a set of quantifiers and qualifiers specific to social interaction. Relationships and processes are intrinsic properties to social existence, the quantification and qualification of them establishes a set of norms, habits, inheritances, laws, "values", etc., necessary for collective life and its reproduction as a society. Therefore, the value is presented as a result of social relationships and processes, from which one can deduce a category of analysis with attributes of clearly historical dimension.

  This brief tour makes it clear that the value must always be understood in two dimensions: 1) as a foundation, an attribute, an essential characteristic, directly related to a given historical time; and 2) as an expression of something, the effect, the appearance, which is manifested by some element (material or not) of general social acceptance. Between the cause and the manifestation of value, in each historical period, there is a set of mediations, in a constant process of transformation, which acts by changing relationships, processes and the content of the value itself.

The history of economic thought reveals to us both the discovery of the law of value, which represents the foundation of economics as a science, and the advances and setbacks in its treatment. It also indicates how value can be both a category revealing the historical nature of societies and an intellectual construction used to justify and reproduce a certain form of production and distribution of the social product.

The formulation of a theory of value was the first step in making economics a science. Although the economy has been recognized as such since Adam Smith, there is still no consensus on the problem of value. At the same time, the problem of value seems to have become irrelevant within orthodox Economic Science. In any case, three distinct strands of economic treatment for value coexist. First, the aspect of the classics for which value should express market prices, that is, a theory of value must necessarily explain the formation of prices in the economic system. The second, represented by Marx, which derived from the theory of the value of the classics, among other things, a theory of the exploitation of the labour force in the capitalist mode of production. Third, the marginalist value theory, for which value is a subjective variable and it is not directly related to neither production nor distribution, since markets are the decisive forces of supply and demand that shape prices and optimal allocators of productive factors.

From the three aspects described above we can understand that the value is equal to price (classic), the value has no direct relationship with the price (neoclassic), and the value as a specific historical form of production and reproduction of social relations of exploitation and expropriation (capitalism). By far, this last contribution seems to be the most promising to think of a theory of value that relates economics and society; and it does not make them "things" of separate existence, as the neoclassical economy itself has done, or simply, make the social struggle around the distribution of the economic surplus disappear by magic.

The great legacy of neoclassical economics and its developments, such as marginal utility, general equilibrium and neoclassical synthesis, can be anything but compatible with any type of society that does not see its own self-destruction: destruction of social ties, because the capitalist economic process excludes much of society from the economic market form, making the economy unnecessary large human contingent; destruction of nature through a predatory process of production and consumption, incompatible with the very preservation of any and all life on the planet; mass destruction by nuclear weapons or by other means and instruments derived from science.

It is important to make it clear that these social and global problems do not exist because of neoclassical theory. On the contrary, being its assumptions balance and optimization, the focus of its economic problem cannot exceed the limits of a choice problem to maximize or minimize a function (consumption or production). It is not that those studies of this nature are not important. They have contributed a lot to the understanding, for example, that profit is maximized when marginal revenue is equal to the marginal cost or, still, the selection of supplies to obtain a certain level of production with minimum cost. They even made neoclassical economics the dominant form in teaching and scientific production in the area. The question, then, cannot be about the validity of neoclassical theory, internally it is valid and consistent, as it is constructed just like a set of mathematical sentences. The question to be asked must be the reason why, even in the face of such a development of economic theory, a historical situation was reached both socially and environmentally. The only possible answer seems to be related to the problem of private appropriation of the social economic surplus and its terrible consequences. The history of the genesis and development of capitalism, described by Marx in chapter 24 of book I of Capital, "Primitive Accumulation", as well as the reports on the exploitation of the workforce, compiled in chapter 8 of the same book, "The working day", leave no doubt about these "terrible consequences", already in the mid-19th century.

Understanding value as a substance and as a form of specific sociability (capitalism) can help to understand both the motives and limits of a society founded on economic servitude and with self-destructive tendencies (social and environmental). Our hypothesis is that value, as the foundation of capitalist society, and throughout its historical development, is delimited from its substance, living labour in the form of abstract labour. In other words, with the expansion and transformation of capitalism, as a dominant form of social organization, the production and accumulation of wealth is autonomous from one's own living labour.

That hypothesis is not original. For instance, Carcanholo (2011) emphasized the character of the "progressive dematerialization of capitalist wealth". For him, from Marx, value is a process (always in development), but for which it becomes impossible to reach its limit. According to this author, the complete dematerialization of wealth would represent the destruction of the use value, that is, an impossibility, because "[...] the destruction of the use value implies the destruction of the human being himself and, thus, of his own value, because this is a social relationship among men. The destruction of the use value would be that of the value, that of the commodity and that of society [...]" (CARCANHOLO, 2011, p. 72) However, the perspective adopted by us is that the dematerialization of capitalist wealth, that is, of value, has a much more elastic limit. Thus, it corresponds both to a process of separation of the value from the surplus value and of autonomy of the value in the face of abstract labour, freeing the process of accumulation of the limits imposed by the material production of the use values.

Therefore, 21st century capitalism assumes powerful new characteristics, among which we highlight: 1) the separation between result (wealth) and cause (social workforce in general), which does not necessarily imply the destruction of the use value, but which makes it largely secondary to the accumulation process; 2) the establishment of a new engine of the accumulation process (digital-financial), which feeds and feeds from zeros and ones, in a semi-closed circuit (intra, inter-business, intersectoral and global); 3) the printing of a secondary character, the production of use values and their accumulation process, which start to serve only as adjustment valves and compensation of financial transactions, legal or not; and 4) the creation of institutions and mechanisms that allow the laundering of large amounts of money, as a substantive need for this new stage of capitalism (although this specific subject is not analyzed in this book).

Francisco de Oliveira was another important author who dealt with this theme from his thesis on "the rights of anti-value", although it is the analysis of an element external to the process of accumulation and reproduction of the workforce, "the standard of public financing of the capitalist economy" during the Welfare State. It represents, in turn, a powerful insight into the transformations of value in the context of the twentieth century. For Oliveira (1988, p. 14), "[...] the pattern of public funding 'imploded' the value as the only presupposition of the expanded capital reproduction, partially undoing it as a measure of economic activity and sociability in general."

The thesis presented in this book is that these transformations in value, as rightly understood by Oliveira, are inscribed in the general laws of movement of capital and its metamorphoses. Therefore, the analysis of capital, labour and accumulation in the 21st century needs to be re-contextualized, because we are facing: 1) a new systemic pattern of wealth (financialization); 2) a long-lasting and far-reaching Technological Revolution; 3) A new standard of automation; 4) a new set of technology-based commodities, sectors and services; and 5) a new state (neoliberal), hostage and commanded by the capital, which acts as an instrument to effect this new pattern of wealth and reorganize social relations to such a standard.

It is also worth mentioning in this introduction "the new phenomena of contemporary capitalism", highlighted by Francisco Teixeira and Celso Frederico, analyzed in the work "Marx in the 21st century". These new phenomena are synthesized under the name of "complex cooperation". Following Marx's methodology, these authors emphasize "complex cooperation" as a "natural" unfolding of the great industry, just as it was manufacturing. The particularity of "complex cooperation" lies in a form of commodities production in which the social movement of capital brings together, in a single existence, capital-money, productive capital and commodity capital; differently "[...] of the large industry, in which capital-money was a particular business of banks; productive capital, industrial; and commodity capital, of traders" (TEIXEIRA e FREDERICO, 2009, p. 109). According to them, "complex cooperation", besides being a less progressive form than the large industry, would also represent the limit form of capital, operating at the boundary of replacing live labour with dead labour. Less progressive because neoliberalism, productive restructuring and social redeemed of labour, as moments of this whole, would represent an offensive movement against the working class, both in terms of the destruction of wage labour protection legislation and trade unions. It can be said, without a doubt, that Teixeira and Frederico were able to update the "Capital" regarding the global process of capital production in contemporary capitalism (digital-financial-surveillance capitalism).

The big question that remains open, which all authors mentioned in this introduction helped to position more clearly, and, which we intend to develop in the following chapters, can be formulated as follows: what if the capital and its respective accumulation process can generate the means of reproducing beyond the boundary of replacing living labour with dead labour? If this really presents itself as a possibility, we can say with great conviction that we are moving towards a much more brutal social context than at any time in human history.

2. The value revolution

2.1. Smith and the value

Smith, in "The Wealth of Nations", by electing labour as the foundation of value gave material wealth an eminently social character. This is an invaluable "value" discovery for the constitution of economics as a science, since it places in man himself and not in an external element, as on earth, for the physiocrats, or in the stock of precious metals, as in mercantilists, the responsibility for the production and reproduction of material wealth. At the same time, as a whole and as a movement, this production and reproduction occurs from specific forms and social relations, established in the context of the material production of social utilities.

However, given the stage of development of capitalism at Smith's time, it was impossible for him to glimpse all the possibilities of its discovery: the dazzle with the fruits of the trade growth, with the development of the social division of labour, with the possibilities of a society driven by self-interest, with the separation between countryside and city; finally, the consequences of the generalization of exchanges and the establishment of exchange value as a social objective really constituted a radical change in the face of the feudal past and became the promise of a new society, based on reason, freedom and the market. The latter, for example, was perceived by Smith as the most important social institution for the construction of this new society. It is not without reason that he has affirmed the propensity to exchange as innate to man, although exchange is not a necessary condition for the social division of labour. In fact, the latter historically precedes the exchange, as Marx (2017a, p. 120) demonstrated: "[...] this division of labour is a necessary condition for the production of commodities, but it does not follow, conversely, that the production of commodities is a necessary condition for the division of labour. In the primitive Indian community there is social division of labour, without production of commodities [...]".

For Smith (1996, p. 85), "[...] The word VALUE it, is to be observed, has two different meanings, and sometimes expresses the utility of some particular object, and sometimes the power of purchasing other goods which the possession of that object conveys [...]". At the first value it calls "use value", and the second value, "value in exchange". For him, also, things that have high use value often have "little or no value in exchange". He cites water and diamond as an example. If alive, he would be awed by the amount of diamonds that the water industry could acquire today, even though the water still has high value of use.

However, Smith proceeds to define the content of the value. Fully implemented the social division of labour "[...] But after the division of labour has once thoroughly taken place, it is but a very small part of these with which a man's own labour can supply him. The far greater part of them he must derive from the labour of other people, [...]" (SMITH, 1996, p. 87). To purchase a commodity from another, an individual also has to own a commodity that has social utility. The exchange will be performed when individuals compare not only the usefulness they will receive from the different commodities, but when they establish a certain pattern that equals in "value" the two different commodities. For, using its rationality, no one would trade a commodity of higher value for another of lower value. This common denominator is, for Smith, the amount of labour: "[...] Labour, therefore, is the real measure of the exchangeable value of all commodities. [...] Labour was the first price, the original purchase money that was paid for all things" (SMITH, 1996, p. 87).

It is interesting to observe the ambivalence that the labour category assumes already in the formation of Economic Science and that accompanies the economic thinking of the classics. The labour, as a term of comparison necessary to the realization of the exchanges; and labour, in addition, productive work, identified as responsible to produce a surplus and cause of the increase in the wealth and well-being of a nation (foundation of value).

However, according to Smith, there is an inconvenience when exchanges are conducted from the comparative logic of the amount of labour contained in the commodities. In fact, it is more frequent to exchange a commodity for another commodity (barter) or for money (society based on production of commodities): "[...] is more frequently exchanged for, and thereby compared with, other commodities than with labour. It is more natural, therefore, to estimate its exchangeable value by the quantity of some other commodity than by that of the labour which it can purchase [...] But when barter ceases, and money has become the common instrument of commerce, every particular commodity is more frequently exchanged for money than for any other commodity [...]" (SMITH, 1996, p. 88-89). The author also cites as disadvantages: 1) "It is often difficult to ascertain the proportion between two different quantities of labour"; and 2) "The different degrees of hardship endured, and of ingenuity exercised, must likewise be taken into account". These drawbacks do not cancel out the nature of the labour as a real measure of the exchange value, only to transfer them to the market that, "not by any accurate measure, but by the higgling and bargaining of the market", adjusts to the equality of values in a way "sufficient for carrying on the business of common life". Thus, Smith, establishes the relationship between value (amount of labour contained in the commodities) and price, as well as establishes the labour as "[...] the only accurate measure of value, or the only standard by which we can compare the values of different commodities at all times and at all places [...]" (SMITH, 1996, p. 93).

Smith also acknowledges that the proportion of the amounts of labour as the only circumstance capable of providing some standard or standard to exchange, is valid only "in that early and rude state of society which precedes both the accumulation of stock and the appropriation of land" (SMITH, 1996, p. 101).

> In this state of things the whole produce of labour belongs to the labourer; and a the quantity of labour commonly employed in acquiring or producing any commodity, is the only circumstance which can regulate the quantity of labour which it ought commonly to purchase, command, or exchange for (SMITH, 1996, p. 101).

Thus, we come to the Gordian knot of Smith's discovery of value as a result of the labour. Despite all the logical paths made by the author, of all the historical examples cited, there is no historical support that, at some point, the value of the labour and its product were appropriated by the worker himself, given that the predominant social relations prior to capitalism were related to compulsory forms of labour (slavery and servitude).

But for Smith it was only from the accumulation of capital or land appropriation that the terms of production and distribution of value were changed. For him, naturally, the value had unfolded into two component parts. In the case of manufacturing, "[...] of which the one pays their wages, the other the profits of their employer upon the whole stock of materials and wages which he advanced [...]" (SMITH, 1996, p. 102).

Of course, he recognizes that the appropriation of the fruits of labour is a social process, this is very clear when referring, for example, to the private property of the land.

> As soon as the land of any country has all become private property, the landlords, like all other men, love to reap where they never sowed, and demand a rent even for its natural produce. The wood of the forest, the grass of the field, and all the natural fruits of the earth, which, when land was in common, cost the labourer only the trouble of gathering them, come, even to him, to have an additional price fixed upon them. He must then pay for the licence to gather them; and must give up to the landlord a portion of what his labour either collects or produces. This portion, or, what comes to the same thing, the price of this portion, constitutes the rent of land, and in the price of the greater part of commodities makes a third component part (SMITH, 1996, p. 102).

Smith, thus establishes, from a logical artifice, a new composition of value, which was once the exclusive result of the labour; and he adds two more elements, the profit and income of the land. In his view, the latter constitute values because "[...] the real value of all the different component parts of price, it must be observed, is measured by the quantity of labour which they can, each of them, purchase or command [...]" (SMITH, 1996, p. 103).

Look at Smith's insight. First, he elects labour as the foundation of value. Thus, it establishes that the equivalence of labour quantities between commodities enables the existence of the exchange, so that the value is presented both as purchasing power and command power over a certain amount of social labour. Then he inserts the accumulation of capital and private ownership of the land. As profit and income of the land constitute command capacity over a certain amount of labour, therefore, too, they should be part of the value. As the exchanges are made by comparing the quantities of labour contained in the commodities and how these quantities are now represented by three elements, no more natural, that the price of the commodities is also constituted by the sum of those three elements. In this way, as Smith concludes (1996, p. 103):

> In every society the price of every commodity finally resolves itself into someone or other, or all of those three parts; and in every improved society, all the three enter more or less, as component parts, into the price of the far greater part of commodities [...] In the price of corn, for example, one part pays the rent of the landlord, another pays the wages or maintenance of the labourers and labouring cattle employed in producing it, and the third pays the profit of the farmer. These three parts seem either immediately or ultimately to make up the whole price of corn.

The theoretical basis of classical economics is constituted, through the value theory and a theory of prices (price equal to value), derived from the former. Note that the transformation of value theory into a price theory is something totally arbitrary, a mere logical device. For, it consists in deducting the value of the forms profit and income of the land, which by entering as components of the price of commodities, are also transformed into sources of value, by the amount of labour that each of them can buy or command.

In this way, Smith not only establishes the elements of the exchange value (or the price of the commodities), but also establishes the relationship between these components and "the different inhabitants of the country".

> The whole of what is annually either collected or produced by the labour of every society, or what comes to the same thing, the whole price of it, is in the manner originally distributed among some of its different members. Wages, profit, and rent, are the three original sources of all revenue as well as of all exchangeable value. All Other revenue is ultimately derived from some one or other of these (SMITH, 1996, p. 105).

It is interesting to note that from a true premise, from labour as a source of value, false conclusions are derived, in their essence. However, in appearance, and only in appearance, they present themselves as true, because they correspond to a given representation of a form of sociability. Thus, perhaps Smith himself believed in the "truth" of his conclusions derived from the idea of labour-value, because they corresponded to a social construction formed from the generalization of exchanges. This construction represented the hope of formation of a society of free and rational men, leaving behind the social forms of slavery and servitude. The basis of this new society consisted of three social classes (salaried workers, capitalists and landowners), and each would correspond to a specific form of income proportional to their respective participation in the social product, so that the price of each commodity would thus be the result of the combination of three elements: wage, profit and income of the land.

What Smith was trying to do was make two things incompatible. Value theory that shows that the fruits of labour no longer belong to the worker, with a society of apparently free men (neither servants nor slaves), in which life was commanded by economic factors, unlike feudal society. Thus, by compatibility his theory of value with the incomes of the factors, Smith places the distribution of the social surplus as something natural of the new society (rather than a social construction from a certain form of property; private ownership of the means of production and subsistence by an also new social class, the bourgeoisie).

To complete its achievement, he needed only to define and differentiate what was "natural price" from what was "market price", thus establishing what would be natural exchange values (prices) or "average" of labour, profit and income of the land. However, in doing so, he also created a huge problem for his successors, including Marx. He established the idea of the need to seek a "natural rate" or "average rate" for wage and profit. In the case of profit, specifically, because this is the variable key of economic dynamics for the classics, deriving an average rate also meant identifying the factors that interfered in it, and that in the long run could lead to the famous Steady State. In this sense, contrasting the profit to the wages and income of the land meant presenting the former as the hero of the new society, which should be defended at any cost, and the latter two as villains, which acted to limit the former, and would jeopardize the dynamic movement of the new economy. Thus, the Steady State is also a logical device, derived from the alleged behavior and the relations that the classics established between profit, wage and income of the land, with the clear objective of defending the capitalist class and raising its status as the upper class of the new society. It is curious that in Smith the steady state has the same cause as economic growth.

In the same sense, we can express the theory of land income from Richard's, by assuming that in an economy already in the process of mechanization (capital autonomy), – in which the accumulation process now commands the markets (of factors and products) and the technical progress –, the distribution between the return of capital and land income was determined entirely by the occupation of new land. He was, in fact, suggesting that the dynamics of an industrial economy were commanded by landowners; or in other words, that the income of the earth constituted the destabilizing element of the system.

Returning to Smith, the distinction he makes between natural price and market price is a central aspect of his economic theory; it is the naturalization of a social construction. It is presented as a logical extension of the labour/exchange value ratio for the entire market-regulated society. The natural price corresponds to the price of a commodity that "[...] is neither more nor less than what is sufficient to pay the rent of the land, the wages of the labour, and the profits of the stock employed in raising, preparing, and bringing it to market, according to their natural rates [...] the commodity is then sold precisely for what it is worth [...]" (SMITH, 1996, p. 110). Already, the market price is the effective price: [...] regulated by the proportion between the quantity which is brought to market, and the demand of those who are willing to pay the natural price of the commodity, or the whole value of the rent, labour, and profit, which must be paid in order to bring it thither [...] (SMITH, 1996, p. 110).

We can find a theory of capitalist economic servitude already in the answer that Smith gives the question he asks himself: "What are the common wages of labour?". After a long tour of the clashes between workers and employers, he concluded that the real (natural) price of labour is that of the worker's livelihood. Because "[...] though in disputes with their workmen, masters must generally have the advantage, there is however a certain rate below which it seems impossible to reduce, for any considerable time, the ordinary wages even of the lowest species of labour [...]" (SMITH, 1996, p. 118).

However, the naturalization of wages contradicts all hope of capitalism as a social formation of free men.

First, because it conditions the wage earner to a minimum participation in the social product, that is, the entire economic surplus despite being the result of his labour is privately appropriated by a "special" class of men (capitalists). Second, because the idea of freedom was directly associated with the idea of self-interest. The doctrine of self-interest suggests that each in seeking his own interest will contribute to a prosperous and harmonious society. Freedom, in turn, appears only as denial of a state of servitude or slavery. The combination of self-interest and freedom are presented to the wage worker as a promise of greater participation in the result of the material wealth of society. However, only capitalists can be favored by this combination, because they are the direct beneficiaries of the economic surplus, while employees are responsible for only the portion corresponding to their reproduction as a class necessary for the production of such a surplus. Therefore, self-interest and freedom are presented only as social constructions; an ideological way of justifying the appropriation of the economic surplus by a new social class.

Thus, capitalism has been presented since its beginning as a form of private appropriation of the social product; its great difference in relation to the previous forms of production and appropriation is in the apparent freedom of the individual, especially the social subject producing value, the waged labour. The apparent freedom of the individual was established through the figure of legal equality. However, historically we have found that legal equality without a corresponding economic equality, in the context of a high development of productive forces, can produce an unimaginable amount of material wealth, however, for the few, and at a human and environmental cost that puts at risk the human adventure itself on the planet.

2.1.1. The natural price of salary

Marx, in "Theories of Surplus Value", Book I, reveals how Smith, in "The Wealth of Nations", was somehow aware that the development of productive forces did not benefit the employed. Such development is related to the establishment of conditions (capitalist private property), in which "[...] the labourer himself can no longer appropriate its result" (MARX, 1980a, p. 48). Smith discovered the existence of surplus value in capitalist production when he noted that materialized work in commodity is divided, in addition to the amount of work contained therein, in capital profit, interest and land income. In general, for Marx, Smith discovered the production of surplus value in all spheres of social labour. However, without making it an independent category of analysis in relation to the special and superficial forms it assumes (profit, interest and income of the land), he could not understand the performance of the law of value in the exchange between capital and wage labour (at the same time an exchange of equivalents and non-equivalents). In the sphere of circulation there is an exchange of equivalents between capitalist and wage earner. The first offers the salary established by the market and, the second, accepts the designations of the law of supply and demand. However, in the sphere of production, that is, in the use of the workforce itself, to that exchange it is revealed that it was carried out between non-equivalents; therefore, the value of use of the labour force produces a value higher than the price it received on the market, produces a surplus value.

The study of surplus value reveals at least four important aspects about the exploitation of labour in capitalism:1) the magnitude of the exploration (surplus value mass); 2) the intensity of the exploration. (surplus value rate); 3) that profit is not formed by the difference between production cost and market price, but by the difference between the market price of the labour force and the product generated by its use in production, which shows the existence of unpaid labour; and 4) that due to the form of property in capitalism, profit, which is a result of social labour and should belong to the firm, actually belongs to the owners of the firm (and thus generates a society in which a few are beneficiaries of all the economic surplus produced socially; while the "rest" receives a portion of the product only necessary to reproduce as a workforce, not being able to take advantage of the benefits that their own labour has produced).

The wage, as Marx explains, still in book I of the theories of surplus value, is not commodity in its immediate form (use value), it is only money, autonomous form of exchange value. The use of the wage by the worker represents only a change of form (M-C), purchase of commodities intended to serve it as a use value, in no way change in the magnitude of the value (accumulation), so that the monetary result of the sale of its workforce fades into the result of its own sale. On the other hand, the use of the commodity labour force, the labour materialized in the product, provides a higher value than the one closed in the wage. That is, "[...] he has added not only as much labour-time as was contained in the money he received, he has paid not only an equivalent but has given surplus-labour gratis – which is precisely the source of the profit [...]" (MARX, 1980a, p. 65). The result of the exchange of equivalents thus results in its opposite, that is, the law of value is repealed in the very result of the exchange of equivalents. However, this real contradiction does not present itself to classical economics as a problem neither theoretical nor empirical. It is falsely circumvented by the idea of distribution from the income of the factors. Thus, the surplus value, as part of the unpaid workday, a constant of previous social relations based on slavery and servitude, was swept under the carpet of Classical Political Economy. However, sweeping something under the rug is not the same as making it disappear. The thing still exists, only we do not see it anymore.

For Marx (1980a), Smith made great theoretical progress by discovering the production of surplus value in all spheres of social labour. However, Smith perhaps was delighted with the results of the development of the social division of labour and the market, by conceiving the surplus value directly in the form of profit, that is "[...] "by thus directly confusing surplus-value with profit and profit with surplus-value, he is upsetting the law of the origin of surplus-value which he has just established [...]" (MARX, 1980a, 69).

2.2. The value in Marx

Marx's priceless value is that he not only saw the overhang under the carpet of the classics. He lifted the rug, put the problem in evidence, analyzed its nature and the consequences of its existence. Marx's value theory presents itself as the most powerful theoretical construct ever formulated to account for the nature of the functioning and reproduction of a specific social form, capitalism. Its recognition of this social formation as the most developed ever created by man (in the sense of the extraordinary achievement reached by the productive forces of their time), did not prevent him from denouncing that this same development was the result of new and more sophisticated forms of labour exploitation, provided by the social capital relationship.

Value and capital as central categories of economic science are treated by Marx as what they really are: forms of social relations established in the context of the generalization of market exchanges, in their determinations and determinants (social division of labour, transformation of productive organization and production processes, specialization, field-city separation etc.); that do not exclude private appropriation of the economic surplus, only convert previous social relations (slavery and servitude) to a new form (wage labour). Like the old forms, it is also based on the economic exploitation of the workforce.

Capital is not born a thing. It originates from specific social relations of production, determined by circumstances of a specific historical time. However, the historical development of capital really transforms it into a thing (abstract wealth), which everyone commands with a bloodthirsty "invisible hand", without, however, ever ceasing to be a social relationship.

The history of the passage from the previous forms (money and commodity) to the capital was formulated with unique clarity by Marx. In a very summarized way, just compare the schemes C-M-C' (simple production of commodities) and M-C-M' (capitalist production), where, C is commodity, C' is commodity with social utility different from C, M represents money and M', an amount of money greater than D.

In simple production the metamorphosis of the commodity assumes two reverse movements in its cycle; and the entire route is presented as the process of movement of the commodities. It is worth noting that the starting point and the point of arrival are both composed of C. At the starting point, C is not a use value for its owner and, at the point of arrival, C is the use value for its new owner. Complete metamorphosis was described by Marx as follows: commodity-form; stripping of the commodity-form (money); and return to commodity-form. Note that the only function of money in this process is to serve as a mere intermediary: expression of the movement of the commodities. It appears "[...] as a solid crystal of value, a crystal into which the commodity eagerly solidifies, and in the second, dissolves into the mere transient equivalent-form destined to be replaced by a use-value" (MARX, 2017, p. 185).

However, money, despite the mere circulation of commodities, is not sufficient for itself, neither as a measure of value nor only as a means of movement. In the development of the social division of labour, and with the exchange generalized (expansion of trade), it assumes the absolute form of commodity and becomes the autonomous value of it (representation of material wealth), then "[...] as a hoard [...] makes its conservation and accumulation into an end in itself [...]" (MARX, 2017b, p. 374).

The development of commerce in the early stages of capitalist society increasingly submits production to exchange value. Thus, C-M-C' ceases to represent and explain the final objective of a society, in this case related to the content of the commodity, that is, the social utility derived from its use value. As a general objective of society, the exchange value comes into force, that is, money converts at the same time into a point of departure and arrival, and thus all aspects of human life turn around this peculiar commodity, money.

It is not our goal in this book to describe the transition process from an economy based on the simple commodity exchange to the fully constituted capitalist economy. This aim Marx has already achieved so brilliantly, including the coverage of the social, political and economic aspects in various passages of the Capital and the Grundrisse, for example. What is important to highlight is that although the ancient world and the medieval world had as a form of economic organization the simple commodity production, that is, they constituted societies in which the use value predominated, there were compulsory (extra-economic) forms of labour exploitation in them. The possibility of using the other's workforce for self-interest appears almost as a gene (born in social groups) and accompanies civilizations throughout human history, before capitalism and the large, mechanized industry this process occurred, either for reasons of little population contingent and/or low level of the technique achieved (productivity), through compulsory labour (slavery and servitude). Then, because of the high population level that we have achieved, together with a highly developed technological level, the process of exploitation and expropriation takes place from wage labour. If we observe, without prejudice, all evolution of human history, we can conclude, without much difficulty, that all possible sociability to date is associated with forms of exploitation and appropriation of the labour of the other by some. The reasons are the most varied: war; debts; trade; theft; expropriation; murder, etc. In any case, economics, as a practice and science, since classical school, with rare exceptions from some thinkers, has become the most efficient tool to give life to this social construct. And capitalism is the most finished, most developed form of exploitation and expropriation of the workforce.

We can say, without a doubt, that the nerve point of this process was the transformation of the workforce into commodity. From this premise we can clearly understand the transition from an economy based on simple exchange to the capitalist economy. And more importantly, it is possible to understand the scope of Marx's value theory (MVT).

First, MVT is a theory about the nature of a particular type of wealth (value in capitalism) not founded on a certain extent of land, possession of a certain number of slaves or the dominion of a certain number of servants. Thus, a wealth that has a life of its own, which has the ability to value itself, regardless of its original composition. The objective conditions for the existence of this type of wealth appear from the generalization of wage labour. From that moment on, there is the autonomy of the exchange value on the use value and the consequent transformation of value into a new social relationship, capital.

The economic value as a result of the product generated from the relationship between man and nature contains use value and exchange value. However, it was only with the establishment of capitalism (with the generalization of wage labour), that this unit was separated to make historically possible a certain form of social and productive organization. Commodity is thus a dialectical unit, a contradiction that moves in real existence. You cannot abandon the use value because this is its content, representing a social utility, but at the same time establishes the value of exchange (a mere representation), as a fundamental form of its existence, regardless of human and social needs.

The analysis of the historical and logical process of the value form is found in section 3, chapter 1, of book I, of the Capital. It is interesting to note that, in section 4 of the same book, Marx already presents a theory of the representation of wealth in capitalist society (the fetishism of commodities), as a warning to the fact that capitalism is a society of representations, where what matters is not the essence of things (in this case, as modern society is founded under a specific type of social relationship of exploitation of the workforce). However, the appearance, reflected in the transformation of the commodity into a social being that commands the lives of individuals, from their ability to accumulate to them, and that although legally free (neither servants nor slaves), they are limited by their respective positions in the social division of labour: capitalist (commercial, industrial, financial), salaried worker, landowner. As already highlighted: legal equality without a corresponding economic equality represents only a more sophisticated form of appropriation of the proceeds of the others' labour compared to the social relations of the servile and slave type.

MVT's starting point is the product derived from a specific social relationship: a side consisting of the owner of the means of production and subsistence; and the other, by the owner of a single commodity, peculiar in its nature, the workforce. However, as we have already highlighted, this separation is not unique to capitalism. In the case of slavery, the workforce is the property of the slave owner. In servitude, the property of the main means of production (the land) is owned by the feudal lord. What makes capitalism a differentiated social formation is the impersonality of social relations derived from the exclusivity of mercantile exchanges, that is, the transformation of all resources, products and aspects of life into commodities.

The 13th century Commercial Revolution in Europe was a major milestone in the long road to this transformation. From the disarticulation of the feudal system and even the formation of capitalism, from the expansion and development of commercial capital and its corresponding new social class (the bourgeoisie), which progressively became a ruling class, in the interval that goes from the beginning of the colonial system to the English Industrial Revolution. In this historical context, the commodity is increasingly establishing itself as the foundation and final objective of social relations.

It turns out that there is a great difference between the commodity production with the purpose of the commercial exchange of its production as a social utility for the satisfaction of human needs. The first function of a commodity, its original function, relates to the satisfaction of human needs. For example, the combination of wood, stone, straw and other elements of nature, through the human ability to build a house, aims at satisfying a need (protection from natural weather). In the context of the exchanges generalization, the constitution of capitalism, as a social organization, such commodity (house), it also aims at the satisfaction of a human need. However, it presents a second feature that dominates its original goal. Produced in a capitalist way, the house does not represent use value for those who produced it. It matters only as an exchange value. The house produced in such manner also represents a form of private appropriation of the labour spent on its production. Since the social relations of production are of the wage-earner type, the difference between the exchange value of the labour force (wage) and its use value (quantity of commodity produced during a working day) represents that the product of part of the working day does not belong to the salaried worker, that is, the economic surplus produced socially is appropriated exclusively by the owner of the means of production and subsistence. The part of the social product that falls to the salaried worker, as in previous forms of slavery and servitude, refers only to the possibility of satisfying the minimum human conditions of their reproduction, just as a labour force, nothing more. Thus, the life of the employed person, as in previous forms of production, must be limited to a labour existence, although now it is in a context of development of productive forces much greater than that of the requirement of exploitation of labour for continuity of social existence. However, this privilege, as in previous societies, also remains a condition for few capitalists.

Commodity, money and labour (their exploitation) are not inventions of capitalism, but it was only with this, they assumed a specific configuration of value. In the social formations before capitalism the value was related, for example, to the number of slaves, the extent of land tenure, the number of servants under the command of a feudal lord. The main characteristic of any product produced, wheat, for example, through compulsory labour, was the satisfaction of a human need and, secondly, to ensure a supply reserve for the following year (safety reserve and stock of supplies). In the context of the generalization of exchanges, the transformation of all resources, products and the workforce into commodity revolutionized value. In capitalism the main function of value ceases to be the satisfaction of human needs (use value) and becomes the accumulation of the intermediary element of market exchanges, money. This was elevated to the category of universal equivalent and became a simple means of circulation, payment and measure of values, in the main element of social distinction, economic power and, consequently, command of the lives of thousands of individuals. Thus, value ceases to be a passive element in the context of human existence and becomes an active element in the formation of social production and its respective economic surplus, a phenomenon that we call a value revolution.

The value revolution has come a long way. In England, for example, the history of its transformations was examined in detail by Marx, between the sixteenth and nineteenth centuries, in chapter 24, of book I, entitled "Primitive Accumulation". Period initially marked by the development and dominance of commercial capital, and its increasing penetration into the productive sphere, also by the destruction of pre-capitalist forms of production (not based on wage labour).

Marx, in this chapter, analyzes the fundamental conditions of capitalist production (polarization of the market among the owners of money, means of production and subsistence, on the one hand, and free workers who have as the only saleable commodity their own workforce, on the other), the genesis of the capitalist farmer, the genesis of the industrial capitalist, the revolutions and the historical moments of the value revolution. He describes in detail, from documents and reports, the expropriation of the people of the camp of their land base (*inclosures* e *clearing of estates*), a "Bloody Legislation Against the Expropriated, from the End of the 15th Century", the colonial system, the national debt system, the modern mode of taxation, and the protectionist system.

The revolution of value has provided an unmatched development in the productive forces, which finds its limit only in the availability of resources of the planet. It has established a social way of exploiting the workforce much more efficiently than in previous forms. If we consider that the original foundation of value is the social relations that men establish with each other in the process of producing material life, we will understand, without much difficulty, all the dimensions related to the revolution of value.

The first of these refers to the change in the importance of value as a social objective. The value of use starts to be configured as a secondary element of life itself, because first comes profit. The second dimension is associated with a production that assumes the dominant form of social relations wage labour. This gives the labour the double character of concrete and abstract labour. Marx called this new social relationship of Capital, relationship-capital, the basis of the capitalist production process.

> The capitalist production process is essentially, and at the same time, a process of accumulation. We have shown how, with the progress of capitalist production, the mass of value that must simply be reproduced and maintained rises and grows with the rising productivity of labour, even·if the labour-power applied remains constant. But as the social productivity of labour develops, so the mass of use-values produced grows still more, and the means of production form a portion of these. The additional labour, moreover, which has to be appropriated in order for this additional wealth to be transformed back into capital does not depend on the value of these means of production (including means of subsistence), since the worker is not concerned in the labour process with the value of the means of production but rather with their use-value. Accumulation itself, however, .and the concentration of capital it involves, is simply a material means for increasing productivity [...] growth in the means of production [...] (MARX, 2017A, p. 256).

In this way, it becomes easy to understand why Marx begins Capital by analyzing the commodity. It constitutes a synthesis of multiple determinations: value, use value, exchange value, concrete labour, abstract labour, capital and accumulation. Let us remember the first paragraph of book I: "the wealth of those societies in which the capitalist mode of production prevails, presents itself as 'an immense accumulation of commodities', its unit being a single commodity. Our investigation must therefore begin with the analysis of a commodity" (MARX, 2017a, p. 113).

Marx's main work is not only an interpretation of capitalism and its form of value (capital). It also constitutes a fundamental discovery about the very nature of this society: legally a society of free men, economically a society of expropriation, exploitation and spoliation of the labour of many (salaried workers) by few (capitalists).

Perhaps the two most important books of all time are the Holy Bible and Capital. By different paths these two works – the first from an element external to man (God), and the second, from the very rationalization capacity of the human being –, seek to lay the foundations of what a truly human society would be.

However, obedience to God does not seem to have prevented human beings from committing the most terrible atrocities against their fellowmen throughout history. In Marx's case, human emancipation, as a goal of a society of social subjects free of relations of exploitation and expropriation, also seems not to receive acceptance. The advantage that an individual can exert over others, over the product of the labour of others, appears as a life goal much more important than the very existence of the other. It is as if the extent of some people's lives depended on the destruction of the lives of many. Marx's demonization is shown as a way to conceal such a discussion.

If we do not recognize the exploitation of labour as the foundation of our present society, we will never be able to establish social relations free of domination and dependence. Thus, it becomes very difficult to hope in a society and in a humanity different from the one we achieve. Even more so in the current stage of capitalism development, by the ease of the workforce exploitation provided by the Technical-Scientific-Informational Revolution, as well as the degree of social control (Information and Communications Technology – ICT and robots, Artificial Intelligence – AI).

As previously highlighted, Marx starts Capital by analyzing the commodity. Not the commodity in its general sense, as a material product of social relations, but as a specific form of wealth of a historically determined society. Hence, correctly, derives the substance of the value and its magnitude, measured by the average labour power of society. This "double" character of the commodity (use value and exchange value) derives, in turn, the double character of the labour (concrete and abstract). It then demonstrates the importance of abstract labour for the transformation of commodity from object of use to exchange value.

Therefore, abstract labour presents itself as a leveler of values, as it represents a general measure (expenditure of human labour force), regardless of the value of the generated use, that is, it is indifferent to the peculiarities of the productive act: "[...] Tailoring and weaving are necessary factors in the creation of the use values, coat and linen, precisely because these two kinds of labour are of different qualities; but only in so far as abstraction is made from their special qualities, only in so far as both possess the same quality of being human labour, do tailoring and weaving form the substance of the values of the same article" (MARX, 2017a, p. 122).

Thus, abstract labour (social labour in general) is at the same time a determinant of value in its capitalist form (commodity) and "property" of the possessor of the means of production and subsistence; the only social subject that can set you on the move.

Marx then begins to discuss the value form or the exchange-value. Part of the simple, individual or occasional value form, in which a commodity expresses its value in a single other commodity and defines the two poles of the value expression: the relative and equivalent form. It goes to the form of total form value, in which the value of a commodity is expressed in numerous other elements of the world of commodities. Then, he proceeds to describe the form of universal value and its corresponding Money form. Its goal is simple, but like everything in Marx, it is accomplished with extreme skill and brilliance. It demonstrates that the generalization of exchanges requires the election of a universal equivalent to make feasible the movement of value (abstract), that is, a representation of this value. Abstract labour content of commodity produced from capitalist social relations (new symbol of material wealth), can now be represented in an element other than the commodity itself, money.

Thus, the autonomy of value is ensured and the fetishistic character of the commodity and the money.

> The two earlier forms either express the value of each commodity in terms of a single commodity of a different kind, or in a series of many such commodities. In both cases, it is, so to say, the special business of each single commodity to find an expression for its value, and this it does without the help of the others. These others, with respect to the former, play the passive parts of equivalents. The general form of value, C, results from the joint action of the whole world of commodities, and from that alone. A commodity can acquire a general expression of its value only by all other commodities, simultaneously with it, expressing their values in the same equivalent; and every new commodity must follow suit. It thus becomes evident that since the existence of commodities as values is purely social, this social existence can be expressed by the totality of their social relations alone, and consequently that the form of their value must be a socially recognised form. (MARX, 2017a, p. 142).

We can designate capitalism as a society of representations, reifications, or as in the denomination of Marx's initial works of alienation: of the commodity as value, of the value as money, of the money as the unique and ultimate determination of human life and its reproductive process. The expanded form of reproduction of such society could not be other than that of valuing value (private accumulation of socially produced material wealth), with all the implications derived from an economic structure that divides the social subjects into owners of the means of production and owners solely of their respective labour forces. As Marx concludes, in chapter 23 of book I of Capital, the functioning of capitalism results in a true law of movement, in the sense of the constitution of an inexorable regularity of such social formation.

Thus, Marx's importance goes far beyond the history examination of the value revolution, which still extends to our days. The work Capital represents the greatest intellectual effort ever made to understand the nature of this new form of value (Capital), and its human and social implications (its undoing of social forms of exploitation of human labour in social relations between free men).

In order to advance in our discussion on the autonomy of value, it is necessary to investigate the productive labour category.

2.3. Productive labour and surplus value

We start from Marx's understanding that value is not labour. Therefore, the "cause of the wealth of nations" cannot be directly based only on the social division of labour. Understanding the cause of wealth requires thinking not in terms of labour, but of the workforce, that is, of expenditure of nerves and muscles during a workday, for example.

In general, the way each worker surplus value to the economic process is directly related to the amount of labour time set in motion. In capitalist production, productive labour is paid labour that produces so much value, directly related to the material conditions of reproduction of the labour force itself, as well as surplus value, directly related to the consumption of the capitalist and the process of accumulation. Thus, Marx (1980a, p. 132-133), in "Theories of Surplus Value", volume I:

> Productive labour, in its meaning for capitalist production, is wage-labour which, exchanged against the variable part of capital (the part of the capital that is spent on wages), reproduces not only this part of the capital (or the value of its own labour-power), but in addition produces surplus-value for the capitalist, It is only thereby that commodity or money is transformed

> into capital, is produced as capital. Only that wage-labour is productive which produces capital. (This is the same as saying that it reproduces on an enlarged scale the sum of value expended on it, or that it gives in return more labour than it receives in the form of wages. Consequently, only that labour-power is productive which produces a value greater than its own).

Therefore, the goal of the capitalist is not the simple commodity production, it is not the commodity itself. This constitutes only the necessary means from which he can accomplish his true goal, accumulate abstract wealth, represented in the greatest amount of money he can concentrate. Asking why this is the true purpose of the capitalist is the same as asking about the slave owner's goal in the ancient economy or about the feudal lord/servant relationship in the feudal period. The only difference between these forms of social relations lies in the nature of value under capitalist conditions and the implications derived from it.

In capitalism, commodity is a synthesis of the production of values, produced from wage labour, by the high level of productivity it achieves – first with the social division of labour, then with mechanized production – it impresses the accumulation process an overwhelming character, because it empowers capital and thus submits all aspects of human life and nature to its incessant movement of expanded reproduction.

Therefore, capitalist production, as so well understood by Marx, is not only the commodity production, but it is "essentially" producing surplus value. In book I of Capital, Marx (2017a, 578), thus relates productive labour to surplus value: "[...] the labourer produces, not for himself, but for capital. It no longer suffices, therefore, that he should simply produce. He must produce surplus-value. That labourer alone is productive, who produces surplus-value for the capitalist, and thus works for the self-expansion of capital". In the same paragraph, he provides an example of surplus value production outside the sphere of material production:

> [...] a schoolmaster is a productive labourer when, in addition to belabouring the heads of his scholars, he works like a horse to enrich the school proprietor. That the latter has laid out his capital in a teaching factory, instead of in a sausage factory, does not alter the relation. Hence the notion of a productive labourer implies not merely a relation between work and useful effect, between labourer and product of labour, but also a specific, social relation of production, a relation that has sprung up historically and stamps the labourer as the direct means of creating surplus-value [...] (MARX, 2017a, p. 587).

Two things are important to highlight from the previous quote. First, that the "productive labourer implies not merely a relation between work and useful effect". The term "useful effect" is very vague, but by context we can infer that it refers to the values of use related to the material existence of social subjects, in contrast to non-palpable use values, such as the example. Second, the generalization of the production of surplus value as "a specific, social relation of production,". However, it seems that Marx did not realize the great discovery he had made. We believe that if he had realized, a part of book III of Capital would have had another meaning.

In book III, chapter 16, entitled ": Commercial Capital", Marx correctly describes that commercial capital is one that acts within the sphere of circulation, that the circulation process constitutes a phase of the overall reproduction process and that, in this, "[...] no value is produced, and thus also no surplus-value [...]" (MARX, 2017b, p. 321). That the sphere of circulation does not produce value is a fact derived from the very notion of economic value, in the sense of value as the creation of a social utility, through the transformation of nature into a "second nature", by human labour. The development of the social division of labour, technical progress and, finally, the mechanization of production make human existence less and less directly related to the direct products offered by nature (without transformation) and, increasingly dependent on the social utilities produced (economic values) by a "second nature" (highly mechanized). Therefore, value production is a specific task to the sphere of production.

However, in capitalism, as the social relations of production are of the wage-wage type, as the use value of the labour force obtained by the capitalist is greater than its exchange value established in the market, the surplus value (unpaid labour) appears as a direct implication of the capitalist productive process. However, wage labour is not limited to the sphere of production. It permeates all spheres of capitalist totality. Since the sphere of circulation is an economic activity in which capitalist social relations also exist, although it does not produce value, it is realized through the use value of the wage labour force. Thus, if the workforce is remunerated according to market prices, it receives a value only necessary for its reproduction, according to a certain civilizing degree. Of course, there are jobs and functions that allow for a higher salary compared to an elementary level of subsistence for the worker, but this does not alter his status as an employed person in any way. We can conclude that although this economic sphere does not produce value properly, only because it is accomplished through wage labour, it does so by producing surplus value. In other words, if the value is directly related to the sphere of production, the surplus value is directly related to variable capital. As the latter is present in all spheres of economic totality, in the form of wage labour, this implies that the use value of variable capital is always higher than its exchange value, which results, therefore, in the production of surplus value. As Marx himself recognizes in volume I of the "Theories of Surplus Value": "[...] surplus-value, whether it takes the form of profit, rent, or the secondary form of interest, is nothing but a part of this labour, appropriated by the owners of the material conditions of labour in the exchange with living labour [...]." (MARX, 1980a, p. 64).

Therefore, surplus value is not only present in all spheres of social labour, but also produced by the totality of variable capital, regardless of the economic sphere in which a certain proportion of it is employed, if it is in the form of waged labour. It cannot be denied that there is a transfer of surplus value between the economic spheres. However, that the capitalist does not appropriate the surplus value he produced, "[...] what They secure is only the surplus-value and hence profit that falls to the share of each aliquot part of the total social capital, when evenly distributed, from the total social surplus-value or profit produced in a given time by the social capital in all spheres of production [...]", as Marx (2017, p. 193), in book III of Capital, becomes a problematic inference, given the finding of the generalization of the production of surplus value beyond the productive sphere itself.

This discovery, in no sense, makes Marx less important; though, it generates a problem for his surplus value breakdown theory. Its greatest importance is in that it reveals a new dimension of his theory of surplus value and capitalist accumulation; much more dangerous to human existence itself, that the mere realization of capitalism as a mode of production that will develop productive forces to the maximum. It makes clear that surplus value production does not directly depend on value production. In other words, capitalism empowers the process of producing surplus value.

3. The metamorphoses of value and surplus value

The value form takes on in the money form its finished figure. Thus, Value Revolution establishes, as *modus operandi*, a permanent search for new means to make the value increasingly autonomous. Process that assumes several dimensions throughout the historical expansion of capitalism: 1) separation between use value and value; 2) separation between concrete labour and abstract labour; 3) mechanization of production and the consequent separation between absolute and relative surplus value, with the election of the latter for constant improvement; 4) as a result of the previous, the separation between value generation and surplus value; 5) the generation of means to make the production of value (sphere of production) a secondary element in the process of capitalist accumulation, increasing the production of surplus value (technological and financial sectors) to the condition of dynamic element of accumulation; and 6) due to all the above, the autonomy of the accumulation process in the face of labour and the production of commodities.

Marx brilliantly summarizes the starting and arrival point of this revolution in the C-M-C' and M-C-M' schemes, respectively. In the first one, the value is associated with the social utility of the commodity as a product of labour aimed at meeting human needs. Wealth is material by its very nature, thus it is associated with physical elements such as the land, the amount of slaves or servants (ancient world or feudal world), as well as the concrete labour these can perform. In the second one, wealth assumes an abstract character of representation. Therefore, with the development of the social division of labour and the generalization of commerce, labour and its product take on another dimension. The labour ceases to have importance only as concrete labour and its product ceases to have as its purpose only the satisfaction of needs. Thus, the labour becomes important not by its concrete result, which assumes a secondary character, but by the amount of hours of labour that can be set in motion and, consequently, generate the greatest amount of the new value, the commodity. Unlike the land, the amount of slaves or servants, in the modes of production prior to capitalism, it is proper to the commodity as a value to move as value that is valued, given the underlying conditions of capitalist production, that is, given the wage labour, which produces both value and surplus value. Using an analogy of Marx himself (2017a, p. 123): "[…] In the former case, it is a question of How and What, in the latter of How much? How long a time? […]". He also synthesizes the transformation of the product of labour into commodity as follows:

> Every product of labour is, in all states of society, a use value; but it is only at a definite historical epoch in a society's development that such a product becomes a commodity, viz., at the epoch when the labour spent on the production of a useful article becomes expressed as one of the objective qualities of that article, i.e., as its value. It therefore follows that the elementary value form is also the primitive form under which a product of labour appears historically as a commodity, and that the gradual transformation of such products into commodities, proceeds *pari passu* with the development of the value form. (MARX, 2017a, p. 137-138).

The development of the commodity form, in other words, the separation between use value and exchange value is, at the same time, the development of the money form. Commodity and money, at this historical point, already function as "different modes of existence of value". This, in turn, "[…] It is constantly changing from one form to the other without thereby becoming lost, and thus assumes an automatically active character [...]" (MARX, 2017a, p. 229-230), that is, it becomes capital: "value in process", "money in process", value "in the process of expanding its own value".

The abstract labour category, elaborated by Marx, reveals the meaning and logic of the Value Revolution. Abstract labour as a substance of value, commodity as its "physical" representation and, money, as an abstract representation of commodity.

We examine three dimensions of the Value Revolution, the separation between:1) use value and value; 2) concrete labour and abstract labour; and 3) value in relation to surplus value. However, this last dimension presents two instances. The first one refers to the separation between value and surplus value from waged labour, which ensures that any working day is always constituted of paid and unpaid labour. The second one is related to the forms of extraction of the surplus value (absolute and relative). In addition, here begins the process of untying the value before abstract labour, both through the substitution of living labour by dead labour, as well as the replacement of the form of wage as the worker's remuneration.

The absolute surplus value is associated with the manufacturing period itself, based on the social division of labour, in which the labour is still performed manually. The relative surplus value is related to the period of modern industry, that is, mechanized production, in which the human driving force is replaced by an external force to man, wind, water and steam, that at the end of the 18th century enabled both a revolution in labour productivity levels (a phenomenon that was called an Industrial Revolution), and the consolidation of capitalism as the dominant mode of production since then.

Marx's historical time, the 19th century, is marked by the beginning and consolidation of mechanized production, which he called great mechanized industry. It begins with the mechanized production of commodities (textiles) and reaches the production of capital goods (railway sector and its productive links), in the first half of the nineteenth century, in England and other parts of Europe and North America, for example. Mechanized production implies a large mass of previous crystallized labour as means of production in the form of constant capital. One of the hallmarks of capitalism is related to the incessant revolution of constant capital that has as its cause the "coercive laws of capitalist competition", which results, in turn, in the concentration and centralization processes of capitals. Thus, the development of productive forces always occurs by changing the level of technique, that is, technical progress becomes a vital instrument of the process of capital accumulation, a movement that throughout capitalism alters the proportion between constant capital and variable capital. Marx examines this relationship in chapter 23 of the book I of Capital, entitled "The General Law of Capitalist Accumulation". For this purpose, he elaborates the category "organic composition of capital", which is nothing more than the relationship between constant capital and variable capital (c/v), through which he investigates "[...] the influence of the growth of capital on the lot of the labouring class [...]" (MARX, 2017a, p. 689).

The capitalism of the first Industrial Revolution, which occurred at the end of the 18th century, from the technological standard of coal, iron and the steam machine, and from the second Industrial Revolution, which occurred in the second half of the 19th century, based on a new technological standard, related to the production of steel, electricity, the internal combustion engine, heavy chemicals, etc., functioned from a specific relationship between constant capital and variable capital. At this stage of capitalism, a part of the constant invested capital transferred a certain portion of its value to the product and, on the other, it was preserved in its former form of existence. In the production process, the workforce set in motion the constant capital, transforming an immovable and constant greatness into another fluid and variable. Thus, the valorization of capital required a certain proportion between the labour force and means of production: "[...] in order that variable capital may perform its function, constant capital must be advanced in proper proportion, a proportion given by the special technical conditions of each labour-process [...]" (MARX, 2017a, p. 291).

From this, in chapter 9 of book I of Capital, entitled "Rate of surplus value", Marx establishes three laws contemplating behaviour and the relationship between these two variables:

> 1) [...] the mass of the surplus-value produced is equal to the amount of the variable capital advanced, multiplied by the rate of surplus-value, in other words: it is determined by the compound ratio between the number of labour-powers exploited simultaneously by the same capitalist and the degree of exploitation of each individual labour power [...] (MARX, 2017a, p. 375-376);

2) In the production of a definite mass of surplus-value, therefore the decrease of one factor may be compensated by the increase of the other. If the variable capital diminishes, and at the same time the rate of surplus-value increases in the same ratio, the mass of surplus-value produced remains unaltered [...] (MARX, 2017a, p. 376);

3) [...] The rate of surplus-value, or the degree of exploitation of labour-power, and the value of labour-power, or the amount of necessary working time being given, it is self-evident that the greater the variable capital, the greater would be the mass of the value produced and of the surplus-value. If the limit of the working day is given, and also the limit of its necessary constituent, the mass of value and surplus-value that an individual capitalist produces, is clearly exclusively dependent on the mass of labour that he sets in motion. But this, under the conditions supposed above, depends on the mass of labour-power, or the number of labourers whom he exploits, and this number in its turn is determined by the amount of the variable capital advanced. [...] (MARX, 2017a, p. 377-378).

The first law establishes that the mass of surplus value depends on the number of workers and their degree of exploitation. The second law that there is a compensation between number of workers and degree of exploitation, so that there is an adequate proportion of replacement of one by another without affecting the mass of surplus value. Finally, the third law establishes that given a certain rate of surplus value and value of the workforce there is a direct relationship between number of workers and mass of surplus value.

Marx was absolutely right in his formulation. The surplus value, in terms of mass and rate, actually behaved in the way described by him throughout the nineteenth century, and until the third quarter of the twentieth century. From there things changed radically under the impact of a new Technological Revolution (based on computers, microelectronics, artificial intelligence, nanotechnology), which promoted, among other things, also a revolution in automation processes. In turn, ICT's gave rise to a new set of commodities, firms and services, which were not imagined possible, not even until the mid-twentieth century, making instant the flow of information, as well as the realization of various businesses, on worldwide level.

In 1972, Mandel published a major work entitled "Late Capitalism", in which he examined the early developments of the third Technological Revolution. Situated by him already from the 1940s, but compared to the present day, it was still only in its beginning. Repercussions that represented the crowning of the second scientific revolution, which began in the first decades of the twentieth century, but which had achieved objective conditions of the "acceleration of invention activity" only in World War II and subsequent post-war rearmament.

The explanatory key that enables us to understand the scope of these transformations, in terms of the autonomy of value in the face of abstract labour, is in what Mandel (1982) called "the acceleration of technological innovation", which we will examine look at in the next item.

3.1 Value, surplus value and automation

In 1867, the year of the publication of Capital, Marx, had already understood automation as an inexorable trend of capitalist production. However, at that time it was impossible to imagine that only 140 years later a Technological Revolution of unprecedented nature would occur and that it would produce a set of machines and processes capable of changing our concepts about commodity, value, labour, surplus value and capital. Computers and cyber-physical systems, artificial intelligence and algorithms, internet of things and internet services, etc., etc.; they began to dominate in such a way the economics, policy and life (social totality) processes, that there is still no way to glimpse the full scope, consequences and implications of this new technological standard.

It is not the objective of this book, we have neither breath nor space to describe and analyse all the changes, transformations and impacts, on the global social totality prior to the last Technological Revolution. We will only approach some of them for contextualization purposes of our theme. Thus, it is important to highlight in the passage from the 19th to the 20th century, the transformation of competitive capitalism into monopolistic capitalism and the resulting imperialist expansion. Major events and transformations on worldwide level marked the first half of the 20th century, such as the implementation of Taylorism and Fordism, two major wars and a global depression, the Keynesian revolution, socialist revolutions (Russia and China), the transition from monopolistic capitalism to monopolistic state capitalism, marking the systematic character of state intervention in the economy. For its part, the second half of the twentieth century was marked by the Cuban Revolution (1959) and the intensified anticolonialist struggles for national independence in the 1950s and 1960s, by the gestation of a new technological standard, the reconstruction of the productive apparatus of Europe and Asia, the crisis of capital at the world level in the 1970s, the consequent offensive of capital against the Wealfare State and the implementation of the neoliberal state, from the 1980s. At the turn of the 20th century to the 21st century, the following stand out: 1) the Chinese industrialization, in the 1990s, its expansionism and project of contesting the hegemonic power of the USA, from the beginning of the 21st century; 2) the financialization-"technologization" of capital and its impacts on the world of labour; 3) the definitive rupture with the Fordist regulation model as a norm of social organization; 4) the global crisis of 2008; 5) the intensification of the environmental crisis; and 6) the 2021 "Covid crisis".

The first step in the automation process was the replacement of the human driving force by a mechanical driving force. The second one consisted of transforming the work environment into an automaton. Processes that are somewhat simultaneous and non-excluding. So that:

> By means of its conversion into an automaton, the instrument of labour confronts the labourer, during the labour-process, in the shape of capital, of dead labour,

> that dominates, and pumps dry, living labour-power. The separation of the intellectual powers of production from the manual labour, and the conversion of those powers into the might of capital over labour, is, as we have already shown, finally completed by modern industry erected on the foundation of machinery. [...] (MARX, 2017a, p. 495).

We highlight four major implications of this moment, three for labour and one for capital. For the labour implies that from then on it will no longer be the worker who will lead the work process, that is, it is no longer the worker who employs the tool, but, on the contrary, it is this tool who employs the worker. The implication of the previous implication is related to the simplification of labour and, consequently, in the expansion of the offer of labour through the employment of women and children. It also implies the replacement of living labour by dead labour, that is, variable capital by constant capital, which makes part of the expendable workforce; which will form a true industrial reserve "army" to meet the objectives of capital in periods of intense economic expansion, as well as to regulate the overall wage rate at the subsistence level. For capital, in turn, it implies a way to produce larger amounts of value and surplus value without necessarily having to increase the duration of the working day. The famous pass from the absolute surplus value to the relative surplus value. Mechanization does not necessarily imply a decrease in the intensity of labour, even because in this case "[...] the lightening of the labour, even, becomes a sort of torture, since the machine does not free the labourer from work, but deprives the work of all interest [...]" (MARX, 2017a, p. 495).

We can also identify a fourth implication that affects both workers and capitalists and has moral content. Mechanization ends up showing the place of each one in the economy and in life. Given the power of the machine, the worker presents himself in "a small and insignificant form". The capitalist, through him, also shows the employer's power the power of boss. It is always more pleasant, despite its unpleasant content, to read this conclusion of Marx himself (2017a, p. 495): "[...] the special skill of each individual insignificant factory operative vanishes as an infinitesimal quantity before the science, the gigantic physical forces, and the mass of labour that are embodied in the factory mechanism and, together with that mechanism, constitute the power of the 'master' [...]."

Marx did not live long enough to witness the greatest advances of the second Technological

Revolution and its impacts on labour and capital. However, its formulations and conclusions are still fully valid to understand and explain the capitalist dynamics of this period, in terms of value production and surplus value. In this period, capital still behaves like a vampire that lives more and strengthens the more living labour sucks, and has in machinery the most powerful means to increase labour productivity; as in Marx's own famous analogy.

The new technological standard brought with it itself an inexorable process of technical and financial concentration, as well as the universalization of machine tools in production, and the requirement of new forms of labour management. In the context of this leap in specialization and division of labour are already put the objective conditions for the introduction of Taylorism and Fordism: the scientific organization of labour that lasts practically throughout the 20th century, and which had become more than a process of production management; it had become the form of structuring capitalism in the twentieth century, that is, the combination of an accumulation and regulation regime that support a set of fundamental macro regularities and a certain pattern of social and economic reproduction.

From 1910, in a context of crisis, the growth and dissemination of Taylorism was considered as an instrument of cost reduction and increase in labour productivity (not without opposition of workers organized in unions through strikes and demonstrations). The introduction of Fordism, a new proposal for production management through the assembly line, consolidated, from 1920, the new productive and labour configuration in capitalism. However, despite the dimension that the dead labour assumes, in the face of the gigantic industrial plants of monopolistic capitalism, the production of value depended, still as in manufacturing, on the living labour and the intensification of its use. In general, the great legacy of "Scientific Administration" was the incorporation of the reproduction of the workforce as an integral part of the capital accumulation process. First, by the generalization of mass consumption by the economy as a whole, opening new fronts for capitalist accumulation. Second, from the 1930s on, and the consequences of the great depression, then with the end of World War II, with the reconstruction of the productive apparatus of Europe and Asia, and with the implementation of the Welfare-State.

In the context of the third Technological Revolution, the period between 1950 and 1970 marked the classical era of Artificial Intelligence (AI), in which it was sought through computational programs, which simulated human intelligence, the solution of any problem. The first physical computer network dates back to the 1960s. Fuzzy logic, which deals with solving complex problems, in addition to false and true values, and the improvement of reasoning automation devices, dates back to 1965. The World Wide Web, though much more recent (1990s), has revolutionized both the way we relate to the world and to ourselves, completely modifying society (digital revolution). The computerization of manufacturing (Cyber-Physical Systems) and the integration of data (Big Data Analytic, cloud computing, Internet of Things, Internet of Services, Additive Manufacturing, Artificial Intelligence, Intelligent Sensors), in what has become known as Industry 4.0, marks a new stage in human history. In this sense, it is a watershed in the same sense as the first Industrial Revolution, which based on qualitatively new means of production (machinery and manufacturing system) destroyed the old lifestyles and in their place, introduced "[...] a new economic relationship among men, a new production system, a new rhythm of life, a new society, a new historical era [...]" (HOBSBAWM, 2009, p. 61). In turn,

> The current process, with the expansion of the internet and new technologies, cannot be taken as just one more step in a series of new products produced by man. As we have seen, the use of scanning introduces a novelty. The entry of these products, in fact, marks the entry into a new stage of mechanisms of production, a new historical period, with a new economic model that guides the economy and social relations (GOLDBERG; AKIMOTO, 2021, l. 1309).

Digital objects do not consist of mere objects of use, nor are they mere finished products of human labour. As objects of use, digital objects do not end in their consumption, such as the commodities of the previous industrial revolutions. On the contrary, its their consumption takes on a continuous dimension in social time and, in the same process, generates both value and surplus value for capital. In turn, the interactions between/among machines, their decision-making capacity, reverse the subject-object position in the relationship between man and machine. Man created technology, but the new technological devices contain in themselves a principle of causality that, from the very interaction among machines, can engender forces and movements regardless of human participation. For example, it is estimated "[...] that about 85% of the transactions carried out on the stock exchanges are today performed carried out automatically by programmed robots for this" (GOLDBERG; AKIMOTO, 2021, l. 1405). The programming itself can become a standalone process from AI, through quantum computing.

The 21st century capitalism, among other forms of designation, also called digital-financial-surveillance capitalism (already moving to a new transformation of quantum nature), is configured by a new mode of wealth, knowledge and power production and extraction. We agree with Yanis Varoufakis (2021), when he states that "[...] for the first time in history, almost all produce free of charge the capital stock of large corporations. That's what it means to upload content to Facebook or move around with a connection on Google Maps". He adds in the same article: "[...] the extraction of value has increasingly moved from markets to digital platforms such as Facebook and Amazon, which no longer operate as oligopolistic companies, but as private fiefdoms or properties", which earned it the title also of technofeudalism.

This whole process and transformation of capitalism would not have been possible without what

Mandel (1982) called "the acceleration of technological innovation", "a corollary of the systematic application of science to production", especially from the 1940s. For that author "[...] the systematic organization of research and development as a specific business organized on a capitalist basis – in other words, autonomous investment (in fixed capital and in wage-labour) into R and D, fully came into its own only under late capitalism" (MANDEL, 1982, p. 176). This phenomenon was determined by a set of factors acting in interaction in the "history of science, labour and society", which link the "increasing acceleration of scientific and technical activity of invention" to the specific conditions of capital appreciation, objectified in the years of the Second World War and the arms economy that followed it. As an example and evidence of his argument, Mandel (1982, p. 177), presents some products from this period as well as the growth of research activity between the First and Second World War:

> [...] The example of the atomic bomb obviously springs to mind, but it was by no means the only significant case of this type. Radar, miniaturization of electronic equipment, development of new electronic components, indeed even the first applications of mathematics to problems of economic organization – 'operational research' - all had their origins in the wartime or arms economy. The so-called synergetic

model of company planning - in which the overall result of various programmes exceeds the sum of the partial results foreseen for each individual programme - is likewise parallel to, or derived from, military programmes. The systematic and purposeful organization of scientific research, with the aim of accelerating technological innovation, was also pioneered in the context of the wartime or arms economy. The number of industrial research laboratories in the USA was less than 100 at the beginning of the First World War, but by 1920 it had risen to 220 remained at this level thereafter: 'Confidence in organized research was increased by wartime successess.' During and after the Second World War these company-dominated laboratories increased greatly in number, and by 1960 they totalled 5,400. The sum total of scientists engaged in research was quadrupled, rising from 87,000 in 1941 to 387,000 in 1961.

From branch to part within the division of labour of large companies, research had become an independent business, and like any other capitalist business, it has as its main objective profit. Regardless of whether their products will result in environmental imbalances, threats to human health itself or even total devastation (a feasible possibility with the existence of nuclear, chemical and biological weapons). Take the case of Monsanto, acquired after 117 years by Bayer ("Bayer: science for a better life"). It produced, along with another major company in the field, Dow Chemical, the orange agent (herbicide and chemical defoliant) used in the Vietnam War. In addition to deaths caused, disabilities, diseases or health problems (related to leukaemia, Hodgkin's lymphoma and various types of cancers, etc., etc.). Do not confuse that with the mustard agent, a chemical weapon used in World War II, which accidentally produced derivatives for the treatment of lymphomas and leukaemia. Monsanto also produced highly toxic pesticides, bovine growth hormone; transgenic seeds. Biotechnology products that harmfully affect health can cause uncontrolled genetic mutations, provoke groundwater pollution, and accelerate global environmental destruction.

A brief digression. Regardless of the historical phase of capitalism, the question of the search for profit as a social norm produces conducts and behaviors of companies to the population, in fact, from human to human, which are of an eyesore for which there is no designation. So the only differences between Monsanto and the 19th-century bakery sector, as Marx reported, are in terms of dimension, technology and capacity for destruction. For, the monstrosity of the form profit is one: the destruction of everything and of all for its realization.

The incredible adulteration of bread, especially in London, was first revealed by the House of Commons Committee "on the adulteration of articles of food" (1855-56), and Dr. Hassall's work, "Adulterations detected." The consequence of these revelations was the Act of August 6th, 1860, "for preventing the adulteration of articles of food and drink," an inoperative law, as it naturally shows the tenderest consideration for every Free-trader who determines by the buying or selling of adulterated commodities "to turn an honest penny." The Committee itself formulated more or less naïvely its conviction that Free-trade meant essentially trade with adulterated, or as the English ingeniously put it, "sophisticated" goods. In fact this kind of sophistry knows better than Protagoras how to make white black, and black white, and better than the Eleatics how to demonstrate *ad oculos* [before your own eyes] that everything is only appearance.

At all events the Committee had directed the attention of the public to its "daily bread," and therefore to the baking trade. At the same time in public meetings and in petitions to Parliament rose the cry of the London journeymen bakers against their over-work, &c. The cry was so urgent that Mr. H. S. Tremenheere, also a member of the Commission of 1863 several times mentioned, was appointed Royal Commissioner of Inquiry. His report, together with the evidence given, roused not the heart of the public but its stomach. Englishmen, always well up in the Bible, knew well enough that man, unless by elective grace a capitalist, or landlord, or sinecurist, is commanded to eat his bread in the sweat of his brow, but they did not know that he had to eat daily in his bread a certain quantity of human perspiration mixed with the discharge of abscesses, cobwebs, dead black-beetles, and putrid German yeast, without counting alum, sand, and Other agreeable mineral ingredients. Without any regard to his holiness, Free-trade, the free baking-trade was therefore placed under the supervision of the State inspectors (Close of the Parliamentary session of 1863), and by the same Act of Parliament, work from

> 9 in the evening to 5 in the morning was forbidden for journeymen bakers under 18. The last clause speaks volumes as to the over-work in this old-fashioned, homely line of business (MARX, 2017a, pp. 322-323).

At the same time of the quoted text, in a footnote, Marx added through the chemist Chevallier other sectors to capitalist "normality":

> The French chemist, Chevallier, in his treatise on the "sophistications" of commodities, enumerates for many of the 600 or more articles which he passes in review, 10, 20, 30 different methods of adulteration. He adds that he does not know all the methods and does not mention all that he knows. He gives 6 kinds of adulteration of sugar, 9 of olive oil, 10 of butter, 12 of salt, 19 of milk, 20 of bread, 23 of brandy, 24 of meal, 28 of chocolate, 30 of wine, 32 of coffee, etc. Even God Almighty does not escape this fate. See Rouard de Card, "On the Falsifications of the materials of the Sacrament." ("De la falsification des substances sacramentelles," Paris, 1856.).

In 1972, Mandel was already fully aware that "technological rents" (capital gains from technology ownership) would become the main source of superprofits, attracting an increasing volume of capital for research and development. However, it was impossible for him, in that historical period, to predict the scope and magnitude of the implications of new technologies, in terms of the creation of new sectors and services, the so-called Big Tech, such as Apple,

Microsoft, Facebook, Google and Amazon, as well as startups (technology-based companies of various sectors, such Lawtech in the legal field, Heatech, in health, and Fintech, in money). We have gotten, finally, after such a long tour, to the last dimension of the Value Revolution in this historical period of capitalism.

Dimension that involves several aspects of this new configuration of capitalism. The first one, related to the creation of a new type of commodity, which produces in its own circulation, both value and surplus value. It is the digital commodities (including the new financial instruments in this list). In general, the *modus operandi* of the new commodities is related to the simple act of surfing the internet or accessing social networks, which generates both a set of data (value) and profit-generating services (surplus value), especially for Big Tech. The second aspect that we would like to highlight is related to the character of automatic feedback of this type of commodity. Once created, using algorithms and AI, these commodities reproduce infinitely and reach new domains of profitability. As a third aspect, we highlight the capacity to master and control new technologies, that is, digital capital (already with quantum-looking), on the material aspects of all economic spheres, the State (and democracy), the world of labour, life itself and its meaning. Fourthly, the creation of new economic instruments, such as cryptocurrencies, which facilitate the circulation of large amounts of money through the underground system, also facilitating the life of tax havens and making various types of crime and violence, highly profitable activities. Finally yet importantly, the generation of a new circuit of capital accumulation that works and moves virtually independently of the real economy. In other words, it has its own dynamics and transforms the real sphere of the economy into a mere trap of income capture. In this sense, the accumulation process (of Big Tech, the financial sector and startups type), in general, seems to hover above the "the law of the tendential fall in the rate of profit". Also because they incorporate in this movement, as described by Yanis Varoufakis (2021), central bank balance sheets:

> That Central Bank balance sheets, not profits, feed the economic system explains what happened on August 12, 2020. After hearing the bad news, the financiers thought, 'Wonderful! The Bank of England, in panic, will print even more pounds and channel them to us. It's time to buy stocks!' Throughout the West, central banks print the money that financiers lend to corporations, which then use it to buy back their shares (whose prices have dissociated themselves from profits).

Unfortunately, we do not have the space or breath to deepen all aspects of value automation in the current stage of capitalism. We would like to highlight its implications, even in an illustrative way, on: 1) the world of labour; and 2) on the accumulation process.

3.2. Destruction of the labour world

Digital-financial-surveillance capitalism impacts the world of labour in three ways:1) reorganization of the workforce by including a new category (apps workers) that is outside any labour law; 2) as a consequence of the former, it establishes new employment relationships with a higher degree of exploitation than wage labour itself; and 3) increases the lower sediment of the relative overpopulation that inhabits pauperism, even for the most workable, definitively launched to informality by new technologies, which both save the workforce and increasingly use robots to perform the most diverse activities previously performed by humans.

In this context, it is not in question just the devaluation of the labour capacity of a large set of human activities, nor only the partial replacement of the workforce by the machine. The era of digital-financial capitalism implies the complete possibility of replacing the living worker by the machine, consequently a complete destruction of the world of labour as we know it. The most intriguing aspect of this process is that it may not imply the destruction of the capital accumulation process. Such is its contradiction! Instead of destroying capitalism, it seems to provide new means to the movement of capital accumulation, through what we call the autonomy of the self-determination of capital. Last stage of the value revolution we will explore in the next item.

Some examples of the former world of labour. McDonald's, the fast-food giant, has begun testing an artificial intelligence (AI) device at 10 restaurants in the city of Chicago, in the USA, which replaces human drive-thru attendants by bots. Another example, still in the food sector, shows that this substitution is happening not only in the service sector, but also in the production itself. The Brooklyn Dumpling Shop is a fast food company that opened its doors recently (2021) in

Brooklyn and operates automatically, with zero human contact. The customer does not find anyone when entering the store, the order and payment are made through a totem, the food is totally made by a machine called "monster", capable of producing 30,000 units per hour, then placed in a closet that the customer releases with a barcode (UOL, 03/06/2021).

Another report, also from UOL, from 04/30/2021, has as title "Without mason: couple will live in the 1st house made by 3D printer in Europe". The first European house produced almost entirely in 3D is in the south of Holland, in Eindhoven, and it was built with 24 printed pieces of concrete by a machine, without masons and a set of materials and structures, previously necessary for the conventional construction of a house. Meanwhile, in Greater São Paulo, Brazil:

> Graduated in Marketing, Claudio Francisco de Carvalho Junior, 37, has made deliveries by apps in the city of São Paulo for a year. He operates in a prime area of the expanded center of the capital — passing through Paulista, Aclimação, Bom Retiro, Barra Funda, Perdizes and Pompeia.
> At the beginning of the covid-19 pandemic, Carvalho found in the delivery an opportunity to remain financially. Today, he says that the difficulties are many, from delicate situations in traffic, the pressure for fast delivery, passing through a remuneration that comes close to dignity only if the journeys pass 12 hours daily [...]

> The motoboys David, 27, and Francisco, 31, [...] became food delivery men because of the pandemic [...]
> Aimless and without money, they bought their bikes, downloaded a delivery app and since then they left the east side of the city every day towards the center of the capital [...]
> Apps delivery men are not formally hired. Therefore, they do not receive benefits such as food stamps or health insurance [...]
> According to the estimate of Sindmoto (Union of Motorcyclists, Cyclists and Motorcycle Taxi Drivers of the State of São Paulo):
> - The city of São Paulo has around 320,000 motorcyclists.
> - In the state, there are 650,000.
>
> The entity estimates that there was an increase of 20% to 25% in the number of motorcyclists who started to work professionally with deliveries and other services this year, compared to 2020 (UOL, 06/2021).

Performing tasks by machines and algorithms goes further. Amazon, for example, has been replacing its HR department by robots, "[...] not only to manage employees in their warehouses, but to supervise hired drivers, independent delivery companies and even the performance of their office employees" (O GLOBO, 28/06/2021). The curious thing is that the report from which this quote was extracted is titled "'I was fired by a robot': how Amazon lets machines decide workers' fate". It tells the story of Stephen Normandin who was fired via an automatic email.

> The 63-year-old Army veteran was astonished. He had been fired by a machine. Normandin says Amazon punished him for things beyond his control that prevented him from completing his deliveries, such as locked-down apartment complexes with key.
>
> "I'm the kind of old-school guy and I give 100% of myself in every job," he said. It really bothered me because we're talking about my reputation. They say I didn't do the job when I know very well I did".
>
> At Amazon, machines are often the boss —hiring, evaluating, and firing millions of people with little or no human supervision (O GLOBO, 28/06/2021).

In addition to the production lines of the most dynamic sectors of the world economy, many other activities have already become virtually robotic, such as call center service, financial, sales and marketing consultants, even commercial stores such as Amazon Go. The latter uses a technology called Just Walk Out Shopping, the same type of technologies used in autonomous cars.

On the rubble of the world of labour stands an unstoppable and at the same time self-destructive capitalism. However, this self-destruction may not necessarily imply its replacement by another form of social organization. It may, yes, at the limit mean the very annihilation of human life on Earth.

3.3. The autonomy of self-determination of capital

This item can be in some ways somewhat complicated and somewhat boring. Complicated because it addresses the separation between value and surplus value from the perspective of section I of Book III, from Capital, which deals with "the transformation of surplus value into profit, and of the rate of surplus value into the rate profit". Boring because it will repeat some aspects of the Value Revolution already presented in the previous items. However, its importance lies in trying to demonstrate that the separation between value and surplus value, the financialization and digitization of the economy, together, can configure a new form of expanded reproduction of capital, making secondary its previous form largely founded on the production of commodities. In a way, many studies have already shown how the financialization of the economy has shifted the importance of material production in the process of capital accumulation. Simply we add to this context the most recent results of the last technological revolution, that is, the first two decades of the 21st century.

As Marx explains in book III, of Capital, the value of each commodity, produced in a capitalist way, is given by the formula $C = c + v + s$, where, c is the constant capital, v is the variable capita, and s is the surplus value. From this formula he differentiates the "replacement value in commodities for the capital value" or "the cost to produce it" or actually "production cost", given by $c + v$. Therefore, Marx differentiates what the commodity costs the capitalist from what the commodity costs to its own production: "what the commodity costs the capitalist, and what it actually does cost to produce it, are two completely different quantities". This difference becomes clearer when the author states that "[...] the capitalist cost of the commodity is measured by the expenditure of *capital*, whereas the actual cost of the commodity is measured by the expenditure of *labour* [...]" (MARX, 2017b, p. 54). Thus, the cost price both appears to the worker as a real cost of the commodity, as "present the false semblance of an actual category of value production". For, if the cost price is given by $k = c + v$, the formula $C = c + v + s$, takes the form $C = k + s$, so k = C - s. The surplus value, s, appears as well as a value surplus of the commodity above its cost price, symbolizing "[...] additional value [...] to the capital expended in the production of the commodity and returning from its circulation." (MARX, 2017b, p. 59). For the capitalist this growth derives from the capital itself, because it came into existence after the production process. Therefore, "this additional value derives from the productive activities which he undertakes with his capital". For the worker, "[...] the variable component of the capital value advanced thus appears as capital spent on wages, as a capital value which pays the value or price of all labour spent in production [...]" (MARX, 2017b, p. 57).

To complete his reasoning, in other words, to show the mystified form of value production in capitalism, Marx initially assumes that surplus value is equal to profit, that is, $s = p$. Thus, if $C = c + v + s$, being $k = c + v$, so that $C = k + s$, and still being $s = p$, so $C = k + p$. Marx concludes (2017b, p. 62):

> [...] Because no distinction between constant and variable capital can be recognized in the apparent formation of the cost price, the origin of the change in value that occurs in the course of the production process is shifted from the variable capital to the capital as a whole. Because the price of labour-power

appears at one pole in the transformed form of wages, surplus-value appears at the other pole in the transformed form of profit.

The surplus value assumes the mystified form of profit and, thus, this presents itself in the world of commerce and production; only as a "sum of value is therefore capital if it is invested in order to produce a profit" or "profit arises" "because a sum of value" was used as capital. Thus, it seems that the surplus value derives from the sale of commodities above their value and not from the difference between exchange value and use value of the workforce.

If, $C = k + s$, and, $s = 0$, $C = k$. Thus, the minimum limit of the sales price is given by the cost price of the commodity; $C = c + v$. In the opposite pole, the situation of the commodity being sold at the commodity value, that is, $C = c + v + s$. In this case, $k = C - s$, implies that being the commodity sold at its value, the capitalist realizes a profit that "is equal to the excess of its value over its cost price". Therefore, "[...] an indefinite series of sale prices is evidently possible between the value of a commodity and its cost price. The greater the element of commodity value consisting of surplus-value, the greater the practical room for these".

(MARX, 2017b, p. 62). Marx thus concludes that sales price and cost price are different things. A situation in which $s = 0$, constitutes a "case that never arises in conditions of capitalist production", as the author himself explains: "[...] It would be quite wrong to suppose that, if all commodities were sold at their cost prices, the result would in fact be the same as if they were all sold above their cost prices but at their values [...]" (MARX, 2017b, p. 65).

Marx, in chapter 4 of book I, of Capital, "Transformation of Money into Capital", formulated his theory of exploitation, thus revealing the full strength of the theory of value as a category of economic analysis. It shows us logically, considering the value as a result of historically specific social relations, as capitalist production transforms an exchange of equivalents into an exchange of non-equivalents, from the use value of the labour force. Equivalence as a principle of exchange is thus maintained in the sphere of circulation, in which the labour force is exchanged for wage. Non-equivalence is an implicit result, because it is hidden in the subtle difference between labour and the workforce; between value formation and the process of valuing it. In appearance, the capitalist made a fair payment, because he paid the labour price determined by the market. In essence, it's a different thing. The use of the workforce during a working day does not correspond to the "fairness" of the market. Because the production of a workday generates a value above the wage established by the market, it generates a surplus value that is suitable not by the worker, but by the capitalist. Thus, Marx formulated the theory of surplus value, the theory of the exploitation of labour in capitalism. See that exploitation has nothing to do with working conditions or low wages. It is related to the difference between the exchange value of the commodity labour force in the market and the product of its use during the production process.

If the surplus value was not explained by the result of the difference between exchange value and use value of the workforce, very appropriately, it would be for the "working time required" to the worker's production and reproduction. It is a clear fact as the day that the fruits of labour do not return to the waged worker, that is, the value is produced socially, but appropriate privately. All that belongs to the worker as a result of the use of his workforce is his individual and social reproduction. Some degree above this condition was conquered only through much struggle of the working class against its total exploitation. However, the struggle between the group of capitalists and all workers represents an antinomy, as Marx (2017a) demonstrated, that is, "between equal rights force decides". So, as force is a State monopoly and as this is a commanded State in a capitalist way, the degree of civilization that can be achieved by capitalism will always be limited by the remuneration of the labour force around a value that revolves around the working time required "to the production and reproduction of the worker". In other words, it is a civilizing degree in which social relations between singular individuals happens from a sociability that always involves forms of exploitation, domination and expropriation.

Marx, also, in book I, presents us a third way of explaining the reason why the fruits of labour do not return to the waged worker. It is the "influence of the growth of capital on the lot of the labouring class", which he analyses in chapter 23, "The General Law of Capitalist Accumulation". Since the production of surplus value is the absolute law of the capitalist mode of production, the form of its reproduction always implies, and continuously, the proper reproduction of the capitalist relationship; "capitalists on the one hand, and wage workers on the other".

> The law of capitalistic accumulation, metamorphosed by economists into pretended law of Nature, in reality merely states that the very nature of accumulation excludes every diminution in the degree of exploitation of labour, and every rise in the price of labour, which could seriously imperil the continual reproduction, on an ever-enlarging scale, of the capitalistic relation. It cannot be otherwise in a mode of production in which the labourer exists to satisfy the needs of self-expansion of existing values, instead of, on the contrary, material wealth existing to satisfy the needs of development on the part of the labourer. As, in religion, man is governed by the products of his own brain, so in capitalistic production, he is governed by the products of his own hand. (MARX, 2017a, p. 697).

If our statement for the formation of surplus value is correct (both from "labour time necessary" to the production and reproduction of the worker, and from the "general law of capitalist accumulation"), the theory of surplus value gains a much greater amplitude than that originally thought by Marx himself. First, because the surplus value is destitute from the value, that is, the surplus value is autonomous. Second, because the surplus value comes into existence in any economic activity based on wage labour, regardless of whether this activity is considered productive or unproductive. From this perspective, the surplus value is no longer a matter of capital being considered productive; it is a question of the very existence of wage as a form of remuneration of the labour factor.

By this reasoning, the difference between cost price and value takes on another dimension, because the surplus value ceases to be an addition and becomes a represented rate in the variable capital itself; whether that rate will be fully or not only the sphere of circulation can confirm. Therefore, $C = c + v + (s/v) \times v$, that is, the rate of surplus value capital gains is intrinsic to the very existence of v. Profit is now given by $p = v \times (s/v)$, and, as in the original formula, varies directly with the magnitude of the surplus value.

Marx, in chapter 3, "Relationship between the profit rate and the surplus value rate", from book III, of Capital, defined the profit rate as the ratio between the surplus value and the total capital (s/C). Nevertheless, in doing so he already defines profit as an internal element, when in fact his formation occurs only through circulation. Moreover, we know that the surplus value is the result exclusively of wage labour. If we want to determine an internal profit rate we should relate it directly to a surplus value rate, as we did in the last formula, $p = v \times (s/v)$. Thus, the variations in p come to depend not on the ratio (s/C), but on the rate of surplus value itself. Thus, there is no surplus value and a profit; they will always be equal within the process. If

v = 100 e s = 100, so, p = 100 × (100/100) = 100;
v = 50 e s = 100, so, p = 50 × (100/50) = 100
v = 25 e s = 100, so, p = 25 × (100/25) = 100.

Marx's reasoning is as if we have two profit rates, one internal and one external. To give consistency to the formulation we have to eliminate one of them. At the same time, we cannot have an internal profit, which necessarily has to correspond to the surplus value, and an external profit, which corresponds to the realization of the internal profit in the sphere of circulation.

From this perspective, too, the question of whether or not commodities are sold at their values loses meaning. All that is important to consider is that capitalist production takes place from the exploitation of wage labour. For, although there is a relationship between value and market price, this is an external relationship to the very generation of value; on which the latter acts as a basis, but also on which prices and their variations, are almost exclusively autonomous, through a competition process or monopoly situations.

The main implication of the autonomy of the surplus value of the value is that there is no longer a need to form a "general rate of profit (average rate of profit)" for the appropriation of surplus value among the various fractions of capital. Although it is still correct to state that there is a transfer of surplus value from one sphere of capital to another. The realized profit in the sphere of production is presented, according to Marx, as a process of adjustment among the different degrees of exploitation of the workforce in the various economic sectors of society. Therefore, Marx's statement that "[...] For each 100 units, every capital advanced, whatever may be its composition, draws in each year, or in any other period of time, the profit that accrues to 100 units in this period of time as an nth part of the total capital. [...]" (MARX, 2017b, p. 193) becomes so disconcerting.

From this point of view, there is no need for the market prices of the commodities to correspond directly to their values, since they function as distinct instances, although related, of determining, respectively, market prices (through competition) and degree of exploitation of the workforce. Therefore, the problem of the "transformation of commodity values into prices of production seems, thus, to present itself as a false problem and, to spare, still does not contribute to think of ways of overcoming capitalism, for us the central question of the unfolding of Marxist economic theory. If value production is both its production and the production of surplus value, all that matters is how much of that surplus value will be realized in the market through competition.

See that this proposition does not deny the law of value, nor does it deny the exchange of equivalents in the market. For, the value is determined by the working time (past and present) and the exchanges appear only as adjustments among the various working times of all branches of the economy. In the exchange between capitalist and wage labour they are exchanging equivalents (wage for labour force), however, from the point of view of value is an exchange of non-equivalents, because the use value of the workforce is a real aspect and not only a fiction like that carried out in the sphere of circulation. The principle of equivalence is therefore at the same time equivalence and non-equivalence. It is not a contradiction in itself, but a dialectical way of establishing the principle. If so, all exchanges are at the same time exchange of equivalents and exchange of non-equivalents. All other commodities besides the workforce must be understood as well. It is in this aspect that the transformation of values into prices presents itself as a false problem. All commodities contain paid and unpaid labour (value and surplus value). The prices established in the market realize value and, in different proportions, depending on the conditions of competition, monopoly or organic composition of capital, surplus value. It is concluded, therefore, that the values do not necessarily correspond to the prices (and do not need to correspond), although they function as their basis.

The law of value takes on a much larger dimension than that one thought by the classics and Marx himself. The distinction between productive and unproductive labour is annulled in favour of the idea of labour and surplus-labour: labour as a need for production and reproduction of the daily conditions of existence and, surplus-labour, as an economic surplus.

As in the classics there was a confusion between labour and workforce, in Marx, too, there seems to be a certain confusion between value and surplus value. Such confusion seems to have as its origin both the distinction between what is productive and unproductive labour and the idea of productive capital. If capital is a specific social relationship between capitalists and workers and, if the surplus value is originated from unpaid labour and, still, considering that all wage labour represents a subtraction of the worker from part of his social product; therefore, any wage labour in any branch of economic activity generates surplus value. That is, the surplus value is a form of existence that permeates the productive capital, being the result of any form of capital. It is not because commercial capital refers to the sphere of circulation that it cannot generate surplus value. The process of circulation certainly, as Marx demonstrated, generates no value. However, commercial capital, as well as fictitious capital, in terms of existence, are sectors in which both labour and surplus-labour are present; therefore, although they do not produce value, they directly extract surplus value from the relationship between paid and unpaid labour.

In this aspect, the theory of value becomes much more general, so that the relationship between labour and value permeates the principle of the exchange of equivalents. In the contemporary economy, in the face of microelectronics, algorithms, in short, the new ICT's, a small amount of labour becomes capable of generating great value and, also, serving as a driver for the generation of other masses of value by other different economic sectors. Even in the industrial sector, in the capital considered productive, the value is produced, by fewer and fewer workers, due to the characteristics of both the work itself and the means of production and digitized organization. Therefore, the relationship between value and labour has been totally transformed, but this in no way invalidates the law of value, on the contrary, it expands its power as an evaluation category of the capitalist economy. Remembering that the separation of value and surplus value consists of two dimensions:1) paid and unpaid labour; and 2) digital technology-based automation (mutually reinforcing Instances).

One of the most important consequences of the transformations described above is the autonomy of accumulation in the face of the production of commodities. Thus, the very production of value becomes a secondary element; all attention turns to ways of extracting surplus value. For, dead labour itself embodied in the technological sector produces surplus value autonomously.

The advance of financialization, in the last two decades of the 20th century, has brought a lot of instability to capitalism. However, as Chesnais (2002, p.

2) points out, "[...] the advent of this form of capital was accompanied by the formation of new systemic configurations and unpublished macroeconomic and macro-social threads [...]". In the 1990s, the financial sector surpassed the manufacturing sector, in the sense that a greater perception of the importance and influence of financial assets on modern economies was generalized. The composition of social wealth, both of families and companies, has undergone an important change with the speed of growth of monetary assets. Movement that resulted from a strong tendency to financialization and rentism and that is not confined to national borders. Process that establishes the autonomy of interest before profit and in which the capital relationship assumes its most alienated and fetishistic form, as Marx explains. Therefore, "[...] instead of overcoming the opposition between the character of wealth as something social, and private wealth, this transformation only develops this opposition in a new form." (MARX, 2017b, p. 498)

In this new configuration of capital and capitalism, the consequences of the last Technological Revolution, of the first two decades of the 21st century, acted in two ways to know: 1) provide stability to the new standard of wealth and the system, through BigTech and other technology-based companies; and 2) to ensure continuity to the process of expanded accumulation of capital in financialized capitalism. Hence, our name of digital-financial-surveillance capitalism. As the authors Goldberg and Akimoto explain to us, (2021, l. 1294)

> [...] surveillance capitalism is not technology; it is a logic that infiltrates the technology and commands it to action. (...) Digital can take many forms, depending on the economic and social logics that bring it to life. (...) That capitalism is a logic in action, not a technology is a vital point because surveillance capitalism that make us believe that its practices are only inevitable expressions of the technologies employed by it.

Thus, we call the autonomy of self-determination of capital the process that results from the interaction between financialization and digitization of the economy, from which a new logic of accumulation originates, which opens new frontiers for the continuity of capitalism as a dominant mode of production. However, the development of this point requires a specific study far beyond what we have been able to implement so far. I believe that the goal to which we set ourselves was somehow achieved. However, at the same time it also leaves open new questions and new perspectives of analysis of the process of accumulation of this historical period of capitalism. So let us move forward, lost comrades!

4. Height and annihilation of humanity

On the edge, we are building a world by machines and for machines. It seems that nature and we humans in general are only inputs now needed, but that we will be in time disposable elements of this process. In the middle, we are moving to make real a work of apocalyptic fiction. Among many others, we remember Elysium, a 2013 feature film by the director Neill Blomkamp. Although it is only a work of Hollywood-style entertainment, it may have captured the meaning and direction that capital society can take. In it, the land of the 22nd century will be nothing more than a large landfill, still miserably habitable by the many who have been left behind. A select part of humanity will live in abundance, peace and beauty, in an artificial satellite, fully robotized, created to be a true paradise.

Capitalism has long since created the conditions that Marx had affirmed as the "Historical Tendency of Capitalist Accumulation", in chapter 24 of book I of Capital: synthesized in the "expropriation of expropriators". However, it did not succumb to them. On the contrary, in only 154 years, after the publication of Capital, this social organization was able to create new forms of value creation, new dynamics of accumulation, new social relations of expropriation and exploitation of labour, which put at risk the human existence itself and the planet itself. By the power achieved by capital with digital-financial-surveillance capitalism, we may never move from human prehistory, in the humanist sense of Marx himself. For him, capitalism would be the last stage of our prehistory, always marked by the exploitation of man by man, and the beginning of our true history, carried out by a devoid class of everything ("a class of civil society which is not a class of civil society") and, precisely for this very part, fully capable of humanity, of the realization of universal human emancipation. Because for Marx (2010, p. 54), "*Every* emancipation is a *restoration* of the human world and of human relationships to *man himself*", that is, the overcoming of his alienation in the face of religion, the State and the economy. Finally, as in an extraordinary way Reinaldo Carcanholo summarized, in his presentation of Marx's work, "A contribution to the critique of political economy" (2008, p. 14): "[...] thus, the possibilities of overcoming violence against true human nature, overcoming alienation and alienated labour would be opened up. One would see the emergence of a society to be organized on the basis of creative labour and that would ensure the full realization of the human being".

So far, all attempts have failed to contain capitalism and the growing expansion of its destructive power. The State and democracy, which exerted counter-arresting forces of great importance throughout the twentieth century, are increasingly powerless in the face of new forms of value and the process of valorisation. The neoliberal wave and the financialization of wealth have once again made the dominance of capital over the State. Democracy is both agonized and manipulated, driven to where the interests of capital well understand. We also had a disastrous socialist experience that took root in such a way in the collective unconscious, creating and feeding a highly negative stigma, which makes virtually impossible any other attempt in this sense. The organizations of the working class, so fundamental in the containment of the power of capital, in the second half of the nineteenth century, and until the last quarter of the twentieth century, were destroyed or emptied. The working class itself was divided and weakened, among:

1) important employees (executives and the like); (2) lower-employed (e.g. civil servants); 3) self-employed, employees through apps (Uber and others); e 4) neither employed nor necessary, nor recognized as part of society, or even industrial reserve army.

The faith of society in science, as a form of humanization or an instrument for civilizing purposes, which was a hope, even if tenuous until the end of the twentieth century, today it is increasingly a sophisticated instrument to stretch to the maximum the social conformism to the world we create. The transformation of science not only into commodity, but into capital, has given this a power with virtually no limits.

Since the *homo* genre began its adventure about 2.2 million years ago, humanity has not taken a step toward itself. Everything it has built was against itself and nature. All accumulated work, all the developed technology, all the produced commodities, were not enough to show us that every life matters, in our short earthly collective existence. What does the degree of education, health, big cities, quantity and diversity of products, technological sophistication that we achieve, if we do not treat ourselves as equals? If we don't do not respect each other as equals, regardless of gender, race, creed, region, culture, etc., etc.! If we and don't we do not share the fruits of our labour as equals!

In this sense, our ability to reason, to plan, to design and to execute, seems not to serve to eliminate violence as an animal form of our existence, only served to execute it with increasingly sophisticated finesse of cruelty. Driven by reasons of belief, race, power, misogyny, xenophobia, wealth, science, etc., the most horrible and great violence, such as crusades, capitalist slavery, Nazism, Neoliberalism, etc., etc., were promoted.

The 20th century is emblematic for humanity. For in just one century, we have created the ability to destroy thousands of years of human existence and its history. The announcement was made in 1945 with the explosion of the nuclear bomb in Hiroshima. In turn, the cold war has proliferated nuclear weapons like mushrooms. Economics and science have fostered continuous devastation on Earth, rivers, oceans, modifying the planet's own biosphere. The globalization of capital, its digitization, and the political form created for its management – Neoliberalism, have made democracies melt just like sugar in water, completed the transformation of politics into a business, by a very profitable way, uniting separating it once and for all from society. There is no uncontrolled development of Science and Techniques. On the contrary, sciences and techniques became capital forms of accumulation by accumulation, completely empowering the capital of the contents of life. The political and social regression to which we are immersed may have a greater meaning; creation of a new society. Not of freedom, equality and justice for all humankind, perhaps only for the small group that manages to leave the planet Earth before its total exhaustion.

As the late Raul Seixas sang in "fool's gold", "I am the one who does not sit on the throne in an apartment with a wide-open mouth full of teeth waiting for death to come". I exist, I think, I write and denounce about our condition. And even though I feel embraced by emptiness. I still do. However, to expect "capital" to change its consciousness and its hunger for profit (that capitalists, in general, develop the awareness that every life matters), it seems to be the same as believing that human history has not been built on the exploitation, expropriation of labour and its fruits, of many by few. In this sense, capitalism would not, as Marx thought, be a point of inflection of this trajectory, but the crowning of the only possible form of sociability throughout human history, based precisely on exploitation, expropriation and predation.

I would like to finish this book optimistically. However, do not seem to exist enough human and social forces to curb the destructive power of capital, as brutal as that of nature itself. The laws of movement of capital have acquired so much inertia that there is nothing else that can be owed its speed and trajectory. On the edge, the destruction of humanity. In the middle, two forms of society physically separated. A rich and technologically sophisticated (who knows on another planet), another miserable, environmentally destroyed and living off the technological remains and discards of the former. Here is our "brave new world" on the way to reality. Capitalism may not be the end of the story, but it may well be the story of the end. Seeing our coping alternatives becoming increasingly scarred is very dismaying, but as long as there is life we must keep fighting. However, scientific exclusionism (segregation of researchers by research group, institution, region) and academic pride (science above society and its daily life) only add one more degree to that dismay.

5. References

CARCANHOLO, Reinaldo. Capital: essência e aparência. São Paulo: Expressão Popular, 2013a. (Vol. 1).

_____. Capital: essência e aparência. São Paulo: Expressão Popular, 2013b. (Vol. 2).

CHESNAIS, François. A teoria do regime de acumulação financeirizado: conteúdo, alcance e interrogações. Economia e Sociedade, Campinas, v. 11, n. 1 (18), pp 1-44, January/June 2002.

GOLDBERG, Leonardo; AKIMOTO, Claudio. O sujeito na era digital: ensaios sobre psicanálise, pandemia e história. São Paulo: Editions 70, 2021. (Kindle format).

HIRSCHMAN, Albert O. As paixões e os interesses: argumentos políticos a favor do capitalismo antes do seu triunfo. Rio de Janeiro: Record, 2002.

HOBSBAWM. Eric J. Da Revolução Industrial inglesa ao imperialismo. 5th ed. Rio de Janeiro: Editora Forense Universitária, 2009.

LESLIE, T. E. Cliffe. The political economy of Adam Smith. London: **Fortnightly Review**, November 1, 1870. Available at: <https://socialsciences.mcmaster.ca/~econ/ugcm/3ll3/leslie/leslie01.html.>.

MANDEL, Ernest. O capitalismo tardio. São Paulo: Abril Cultural, 1982. (Os economistas).

MARX, Karl. Contribuição à crítica da economia política. 2nd ed. São Paulo: Expressão Popular, 2008.

_____. O capital: crítica da economia política. Book III: o processo global da produção capitalista. São Paulo: Boitempo, 2017b.

_____. Grundrisse: manuscritos econômicos de 1857-1858: esboços da crítica da economia política. São Paulo: Boitempo; Rio de Janeiro: Ed. UFRJ, 2011.

_____. O capital: crítica da economia política. Book I: o processo de produção do capital. 2nd ed. São Paulo: Boitempo, 2017a.

_____. Sobre a questão judaica. São Paulo: Boitempo, 2010.

_____. Teorias da mais-valia: história crítica do pensamento econômico. Rio de Janeiro: Editora Civilização Brasileira, 1980a, (Vol. 1).

_____. Teorias da mais-valia: história crítica do pensamento econômico. São Paulo: DIFEL, 1980b. (Vol. 2).

O GLOBO. 'Fui despedido por um robô': como a Amazon deixa máquinas decidirem destino dos trabalhadores. Published on June 28 2021. Available at: <https://oglobo.globo.com/economia/tecnologia/fui-despedido-por-um-robo-como-amazon-deixa-maquinas-decidirem-destino-dos-trabalhadores-25079925>.
Accessed on July 15 2021.

OLIVEIRA, Francisco. O surgimento do antivalor: capital, força de trabalho e fundo público. São Paulo: **Novos Estudos**, n. 22, October, 1988.

RICARDO, David. Princípios de Economia política e tributação. São Paulo: Abril Cultural, 1982. (Os economistas).

ROTHSCHILD, Emma. Sentimentos econômicos: Adam Smith, Condorcet e o Iluminismo. Rio de Janeiro: Record, 2003.

SMITH, Adam. A riqueza das nações: investigação sobre sua natureza e causas. São Paulo: Editora Nova Cultural Ltda, 1996. (Os economistas, vol. I).

TEIXEIRA, Francisco José Soares. Trabalho e valor: contribuição para a crítica da razão econômica. São Paulo: Cortez Editora, 2004.

_____. FREDERICO, Celso. Marx no século XXI. 2nd ed. São Paulo: Cortez, 2009.

UOL. "Almoçar é uma raridade". Published on June 2021. Available at: <https://noticias.uol.com.br/reportagens-especiais/desigualdade-na-pandemia---na-rua-e-com-fome/#cover>. Accessed on July 15 2021.

UOL. "Robô 'monstro' produz 500 refeições por minuto em novo fast-food de NY". Published on June 03 2021. Available at: <https://www.uol.com.br/nossa/noticias/redacao/2021/06/03/novo-fast-food-automatico-produz-500-dumplings-por-minuto-sem-funcionarios.htm?cmpid=copiaecola>. Accessed on July 15 2021.

UOL. "Sem pedreiro: casal vai viver na 1ª casa feita por impressora 3D na Europa". Published on April 30 2021. Available at: <https://www.uol.com.br/tilt/noticias/redacao/2021/04/30/sem-pedreiro-casal-vai-viver-em-casa-totalmente-feita-por-impressora-3d.htm?cmpid=copiaecola>. Accessed on July 15 2021.

VAROUFAKIS, Yanis. O tecnofeudalismo está assumindo o controle. Published on the website **a terra é redonda**, on July 02 2021. Available at: <https://aterraeredonda.com.br/o-tecnofeudalismo-esta-assumindo-o-controle/>. Accessed on July 12 2021.

www.ingramcontent.com/pod-product-compliance
Lightning Source LLC
Chambersburg PA
CBHW031426210526
45464CB00005B/2072